This book is to be returned on or before the last date below.

947.084

19 SEP 1997

16 OCT 1997

23 JAN 1998

-6 SEP 1999

-8 FEB 2000

29 FEB 2000

1 2 OCT 2010

DOCUMENTS AND DEBATES

The original titles in the series (still available):

Sixteenth Century England 1450–1600	Denys Cook
Sixteenth Century Europe	Katherine Leach
Seventeenth Century Britain	John Wroughton
Seventeenth Century Europe	Gary Martin Best
Eighteenth Century Europe	L.W. Cowie
Nineteenth Century Britain	Richard Brown and Christopher Daniels
British Social and Economic History 1800–1900	Neil Tonge and Michael Quincey
Nineteenth Century Europe	Stephen Brooks
Twentieth Century Europe	Richard Brown and Christopher Daniels
Twentieth Century Britain	Richard Brown and Christopher Daniels

For the extended series, see the back of this book.

Documents and Debates
General Editor: John Wroughton M.A., F.R.Hist.S.

The Russian Revolution

Niall Rothnie
Head of History, King Edward VI School, Bath

MACMILLAN

First published 1990 by
THE MACMILLAN PRESS LTD
Houndmills, Basingstoke, Hampshire RG21 2XS
and London
Companies and representatives
throughout the world

ISBN 0–333–46735–3

A catalogue record for this book is available
from the British Library.

Printed in Malaysia

11 10   9   8   7   6   5   4   3
03 02 01 00 99 98 97 96 95

Contents

	General Editor's Preface	vii
	Acknowledgements	viii
	Introduction	1
I	Russian Political Parties: Theory and Practice	5
II	The February Revolution	23
III	The Provisional Government (i) February–June	40
IV	The Provisional Government (ii) July–October	56
V	The October Revolution	72
VI	Civil War	87
VII	Domestic Policy	104
VIII	The Last Years of Lenin	119

To Fiona Wylie

General Editor's Preface

This book forms part of a series entitled *Documents and Debates*, which is aimed primarily at sixth formers. The earlier volumes in the series each covered approximately one century of history, using material both from original documents and from modern historians. The more recent volumes, however, are designed in response to the changing trends in history examinations at 18 plus, most of which now demand the study of documentary sources and the testing of historical skills. Each volume therefore concentrates on a particular topic within a narrow span of time. It consists of eight sections, each dealing with a major theme in depth, illustrated by extracts drawn from primary sources. The series intends partly to provide experience for those pupils who are required to answer questions on documentary material at A-level, and partly to provide pupils of all abilities with a digestible and interesting collection of source material, which will extend the normal textbook approach.

This book is designed essentially for the pupil's own personal use. The author's introduction will put the period as a whole into perspective, highlighting the central issues, main controversies, available source material and recent developments. Although it is clearly not our intention to replace the traditional textbook, each section will carry its own brief introduction, which will set the documents into context. A wide variety of source material has been used in order to give the pupils the maximum amount of experience – letters, speeches, newspapers, memoirs, diaries, official papers, Acts of Parliament, Minute Books, accounts, local documents, family papers, etc. The questions vary in difficulty, but aim throughout to compel the pupil to think in depth by the use of unfamiliar material. Historical knowledge and understanding will be tested, as well as basic comprehension. Pupils will also be encouraged by the questions to assess the reliability of evidence, to recognise bias and emotional prejudice, to reconcile conflicting accounts and to extract the essential from the irrelevant. Some questions, *marked with an asterisk*, require knowledge outside the immediate extract and are intended for further research or discussion, based on the pupil's general knowledge of the period. Finally, we hope that students using this material will learn something of the nature of historical inquiry and the role of the historian.

John Wroughton

Acknowledgements

The author and publishers wish to thank the following for permission to use copyright material: Chapman and Hall for extracts from *Russia's Ruin* by E. H. Wilcox, 1919; Curtis Brown Group Ltd. on behalf of the Estate of Winston S. Churchill for extracts from *The Aftermath* by Winston S. Churchill, Macmillan & Co., 1941 Copyright © 1941 The Estate of Sir Winston Churchill and the Hamlyn Group Ltd; Macmillan, London and Basingstoke for extracts from *Memoirs of a British Agent* by R. H. Lockhart, 1974; Oxford University Press for extracts from *The Russian Revolution 1917: A Personal Record* by N. N. Sukhanov, edited and translated by Joel Carmichael, 1955; Stanford University Press for extracts from *The Bolshevik Revolution, 1917–1918* by James Bunyan and H. H. Fisher: Copyright © 1934, renewed 1961 by the Board of Trustees of the Leland Stanford Junior University; The University of Michigan Press for extracts from *The History of the Russian Revolution* by Leon Trotsky, translated by Max Eastman, 1932–33, published in paperback by Monad Press, 1980.

Every effort has been made to trace all the copyright holders, but if any have been inadvertently overlooked the publishers will be pleased to make the necessary arrangement at the first opportunity.

Introduction

It is perhaps indicative of the continuing interest in the Russian Revolution that at least half of the extracts quoted in this book were found in the politics sections of libraries rather than under history. Seventy years on, the revolution is still seen as contemporary history, and certainly not as something that is long dead and finished.

In many ways there is a profusion of sources on the subject, not least from the main participants in the events. Long years in exile with a great deal of spare time and interminable meetings appear to have created a mania for writing, a habit that did not end when the Bolsheviks came to power: Trotsky was writing his massive history of the revolution whilst directing the civil war. Nor, at first, was secrecy of paramount importance. Kamanev and Zinoviev announced their opposition to the timing of the October Revolution in a Bolshevik newspaper and before the actual event. Lenin wrote a great deal, and his collected works are readily available in English translation, published in Russia and massively subsidised. While in exile from the late 1920s onwards, Trotsky spent even more time in writing articles, memoirs and attacks on Stalin. The same is also true of many leading opponents of the Bolsheviks. During the revolutionary years most Russian political leaders went into exile; it was not until Stalin's rule that individuals tended to meet a more final punishment for daring to oppose the government. Thus we have biographies and memoirs of many important Russians: Chernov of the Social Revolutionaries, Miliukov for the Cadets, Sukhanov and the Mensheviks. Alexander Kerensky, last leader of the Provisional Government, seems to have been affected by the same desire for literary immortality as the Bolsheviks he opposed. In the first months after his downfall in October 1917 he was already rushing into print to explain why he fell from power. He lived a very long time afterwards and continued to produce regular apologies for his actions.

During the revolutionary years Russia also appears to have been populated by a large number of foreign observers. Both French and British ambassadors put their experiences into print, followed closely by assorted lesser officials as well as a wide variety of what might be loosely termed government agents. The Bolsheviks liked to stress the international aspects of their revolution as well as their desire to maintain close links between themselves and the people. Foreign journalists found it relatively easy to visit Russia and meet its leaders. It helped, of course, if one showed a certain sympathy for the Bolsheviks in the first place, as did the American socialist John Reed, perhaps the most famous of the foreign observers at this time. The keen reporter had many other sources. The many and partisan Russian newspapers also printed a great deal of information: manifestos and proclamations of parties, and the evidence of factional disputes as revealed by the letters pages of the popular journals.

However, this mass of information is far from being the whole story. Russia remains one of the few countries in the world where the nearer one gets to the present, the less information is available. There is certainly more on the Provisional Government than on the first years of Bolshevik rule and far more than on Stalin's rule of the 1930s. As communist control became more secure and firmer there were fewer leaks on party policy and divisions until observers were reduced to estimating the positions of power by watching who stood where on the dais of Lenin's tomb on the great May Day and October Revolution celebrations. Why did control of information become so strict? To answer this question one must remember two points. Communism does not believe in pluralism: there is only ever one proper course of action and communism holds a monopoly of the truth. Communist governments do not make mistakes (or, at least, they rarely admit to them). Unfortunately the gurus of communism, reduced once more to Marx and Lenin, were rarely specific and never all-embracing. New problems arise that they did not consider and, like the Bible, different groups can argue different interpretations of key phrases, especially if they are taken out of context. The struggle for power between Trotsky and Stalin in the 1920s depended to a large extent on which of them could prove he was the true interpreter of Lenin's views. Combine these two factors – that in theory communism is always correct, but in practice its founding fathers often made omissions and have subsequently been proved wrong – and then one should hardly expect the present Russian authorities to print everything. In extreme cases, communists who have subsequently proved an embarrassment to the Social Government have officially ceased to exist. Stalin erased records of practically every surviving Bolshevik leader during his purges of the 1930s. Trotsky at least fled abroad and had a few years to write his memoirs before he was tracked down and killed in Mexico in 1940. Others were less lucky. Zinoviev, Kamanev, Bukharin, Rykov, Tomsk, a long line of key communist personnel had no opportunity to record their views for posterity.

In turn, Stalin himself was posthumously disgraced. Unlike the people he had previously liquidated, his writings had been published, but they are no longer available in Russia. The extracts included in this book are taken from English translations published in China as that country did not follow Russia's lead in declaring Stalin a non-person. Lenin has never been out of fashion. It would take an historian of rare persistence to study all of the supposed Collected Works of Lenin published in Moscow to see whether some, detrimental to the great leader, have been omitted; but this, perhaps, is not the point. These are the collected printed works, articles, pamphlets and minutes of public meetings. Private gatherings and personal notes are not available to us. One must always remember in studying official documents and pamphlets from Soviet sources that they are just that – official sources. One is left with the impression throughout the revolutionary period, of a vast and monolithic Communist Party, united on policy, dominated by the brilliance of Lenin. We see what the Soviet government want us to see.

This naturally raises the question of the availability of non-official sources, those sometimes hostile to the communists. It must be said that the published memoirs of other Russian politicians are generally something of a disappointment. It is not just that Kerensky, Miliukov and the others were obsessed with simply proving that they were right. Most were also writing years after the event and in exile, with little access to the official records of the time. This is the greatest gap in our knowledge. There is little hope of the present government in Russia ever opening up the state archives of seventy years ago. This is, perhaps, not as crucial as it might first appear. There are few real mysteries concerning the events of 1917–24. Most historians agree on the general causes of the tsar's downfall, the rise and collapse of the Provisional Government, the Bolshevik seizure of power. The controversies are relatively minor: quite what Kornilov was trying to achieve in his abortive coup and the evergreen mystery concerning the fate of the odd member of the tsar's family. But without the official records we are still forced to accept a rather non-critical view of the Bolshevik government without being able to check on its mistakes, its support (or lack thereof) and, in particular, the records of its opponents. The greater problem for the average student of the Russian Revolution is his own attitude. There is a strong argument that says we have always been suspicious of Russia because of its sheer size and autocratic style of government. Others argue that it was only the creation of a communist government that sowed the seeds of mutual distrust between West and East. Western historians, accustomed to free speech and a choice of political parties, look askance at communist Russia. They tend to support those Russians who had most in common with the West.

Thus the Provisional Government in general and Kerensky in particular have attracted much favourable comment. This fact must be remembered; a deep distrust of Russia today hardly gives one the open mind necessary for the study of this period.

The layout of this book follows a broad chronological order. It begins with Karl Marx and communism, as Russia had one of the first revolutions where the leaders followed not just their own ideas, but also the writings of nineteenth-century theorists. It then looks at the end of the tsarist rule, the period of the Provisional Government and the seizure of power by the Bolsheviks in October 1917. The problems faced by the new rulers are looked at in relation to active opposition from other parties and factions as well as their own new policies. The book concludes with the death of Lenin in early 1924. It can be argued that this is a rather artificial end, brought on largely by the need to give sufficient depth to a restricted period. Lenin had only recently introduced the New Economic Policy, a retreat from basic communist beliefs. Communism did not just mean a change of government but also a change of hearts and minds in Russian society. According to Marxist theory, once people had been forced to be free and to share, then the strong government, the dictatorship of the proletariat, would fade away. In that case the revolution is still not complete, for the government has most certainly not voted itself out of existence. Some critics would argue this merely shows that the Russians are not true Communists. Others claim it proves that communism does not work. Marx himself took an optimistic view of human nature. He felt that once the evil influence of capitalism had been removed then people would be prepared to share and to work together. Perhaps we have just failed to live up to Marx's own high-minded beliefs.

I Russian Political Parties: Theory and Practice

Introduction

Marx accepted the traditional communist view that private property should be abolished and that everything be held in communal ownership. His personal contribution was to construct a theoretical framework to show that the state of communism was both natural and inevitable. Unnatural greed led everyone to attempt to become wealthier but at present this meant that the few had much and the many had little. Marx suggested the idea of class struggle, that there were three classes each seeking the dominant position in society. As economic strength inevitably flowed from one class to the next, then the class structure changed as well. The feudal classes would inevitably be supplanted by the bourgeoisie, or middle class, and these in turn by the proletariat, or workers, who would then set up a strong but temporary government, the dictatorship of the proletariat, to rid people of their greed and force them to share. This having been accomplished, the central state power could simply wither away.

None of this seemed relevant to nineteenth-century Russia which was predominantly agricultural with few members of the middle classes, let alone the workers. The Russian communist party, the Social Democrats, was thus of marginal importance. It caused further problems for itself in the early 1900s when it split over rival interpretations of Marx. The Bolsheviks, under Lenin, were criticised for changing Marx's ideas to fit in with the particular circumstances in Russia; the need for secret rather than open leadership and the need to appeal to the peasants. The Mensheviks believed they adhered more fully to Marx's basic tenets of a relatively open and tolerant party that accepted a slow development of the proletariat after the bourgeoisie had come to power.

Potentially the strongest party in Russia was the Social Revolutionaries who were also socialist in outlook but inspired not by the West, Marx and industry but by Russia itself. Their hope lay in a misty and vague communism based on the peasants although they also felt that the assassination of key personnel could hasten the government's downfall.

The party that had most in common with western liberals was

the Constitutional Democrats, or Cadets. They were doubly handicapped both by the lack of a strong middle class in Russia and the fact that it was impossible to be a moderate in opposition to the tsar when he allowed no organised opposition at all.

At the end of the nineteenth century it could not be said that any of the above named parties had any real importance in Russia at all.

1   Marxist Theory

(a) An economic theory of history

The materialist conception of history starts from the proposition that the production of the means to support human life and, next to production, the exchange of things produced, is the basis of all social structure; that in every society that has appeared in history,
5 the manner in which wealth is distributed and society divided into classes or orders is dependent upon what is produced, how it is produced, and how the products are exchanged. From this point of view the final causes of all social changes and political revolutions are to be sought, not in men's brains, not in man's better insight
10 into eternal truth and justice, but in changes in the modes of production and exchange. They are to be sought, not in the philosophy, but in the economics of each particular epoch. The growing perception that existing social institutions are unreasonable and unjust, that reason has become unreason and right wrong, is
15 only proof that in the modes of production and exchange changes have silently taken place with which the social order, adapted to earlier economic conditions, is no longer in keeping. From this it also follows that the means of getting rid of the incongruities that have been brought to light must also be present, in a more or less
20 developed condition, within the changed modes of production themselves. These means are not to be invented by deduction from fundamental principles, but are to be discovered in the stubborn facts of the existing system of production.

> Marx–Engels, *Selected Works*, vol 2 (Moscow, 1950). Quoted in Sidney Hook, *Marx and the Marxists* (Princeton, NJ, 1955)

(b) The individual in history

The same thing may be said about Robespierre. Let us assume that
25 he was an absolutely indispensable force in his party; but at all events, he was not the only force. If the accidental fall of a brick had killed him, say, in January, 1793, his place would, of course, have been taken by somebody else, and although this person might have been inferior to him in every respect, nevertheless, events

30　would have taken the same course as they did when Robespierre
was alive. For example, even under these circumstances the Gironde
would probably not have escaped defeat; but it is possible that
Robespierre's party would have lost power somewhat earlier and
we would now be speaking not of the Thermidor reaction, but of
35　the Floréal, Prairial or Messidor reaction. Perhaps some will say
that with his inexorable terror, Robespierre did not delay but
hastened the downfall of his party. We will not stop to examine
this supposition here; we will accept it as if it were quite sound. In
that case we must assume that Robespierre's party would have fallen
40　not in Thermidor, but in Fructidor, Vendémaire, or Brumaire. In
short, it may have fallen sooner or perhaps later, but it certainly
would have fallen, because the section of the people which supported
Robespierre's party was totally unprepared to hold power for a
prolonged period. At all events, results 'opposite' to those which
45　arose from Robespierre's energetic action are out of the question.

G. V. Plekhanov, *The Role of the Individual in History*
(Moscow, 1944) pp 40–1

Questions

a　In extract (a) what is the materialist conception of history?
b　According to this extract, at what stage do people begin to
question the existence of present social institutions?
c　How important was Robespierre to the French Revolution,
according to extract (b)?
d　Compare extracts (a) and (b). Why does the individual play
only a limited role in history?

(c) The class struggle

The history of all hitherto existing society is the history of class
struggles.

Freeman and slave, patrician and plebian, lord and serf, guild-
master and journeyman, in a word, oppressor and oppressed, stood
5　in constant opposition to one another, carried on an uninterrupted,
now hidden, now open fight, a fight that each time ended, either
in a revolutionary reconstitution of society at large, or in the
common ruin of the contending classes.

The modern bourgeois society that has sprouted from the ruins
10　of feudal society has not done away with class antagonisms. It has
but established new classes, new conditions of oppression, new
forms of struggle in place of the old ones. Our epoch, the epoch
of the bourgeoisie, possesses, however, this distinctive feature: it
has simplified the class antagonisms. Society as a whole is more
15　and more splitting up into two great hostile camps, into two great
classes directly facing each other: Bourgeoisie and Proletariat.

From the serfs of the Middle Ages sprang the chartered burghers of the earliest towns. From these burgesses the first elements of the bourgeoisie were developed.

20 . . . At a certain stage in the development of these means of production and of exchange, the conditions under which feudal organization of agriculture and manufacturing industry, in one word, the feudal relations of property became no longer compatible with the already developed productive forces; they become so many
25 fetters. They had to be burst asunder, they were burst asunder.

Into their place stepped free competition, accompanied by a social and political constitution adapted to it, and by the economical and political sway of the bourgeois class.

A similar movement is going on before our own eyes. Modern
30 bourgeois society with its relations of production, of exchange and of property, a society that has conjured up such gigantic means of production and of exchange, is like the sorcerer, who is no longer able to control the powers of the nether world whom he has called up by his spells. . . .

35 By bourgeoisie is meant the class of modern Capitalists, owners of the means of social production and employers of wage labour. By proletariat, the class of modern wage-labourers who, having no means of production of their own, are reduced to selling their labour power in order to live. (Note by Engels to the English
40 edition of 1888.)

Karl Marx and Friedrich Engels, *The Communist Manifesto* (1979) pp 80–1, 85, 89

(d) The Workers Revolution

The transformation of the individualised and scattered means of production into socially concentrated ones, of the pigmy property of the many into the huge property of the few, the expropriation of the great mass of the people from the soil, from the means of
45 subpainful expropriation of the mass of people forms the prelude to the history of capital. Self-earned private property, that is based, so to say, on the fusing together of the isolated, independent labourer with the conditions of his labour, is supplanted by capitalistic private property, which rests on exploitation of the
50 nominally free labour of others, i.e., on wages–labour.

As soon as this process of transformation has sufficiently decomposed the old society from top to bottom, as soon as the labourers are turned into proletarians, their means of labour into capital, as soon as the capitalist mode of production stands on its own
55 feet, then the further socialisation of labour and the further transformation of the land and other means of production, as well as the further expropriation of private properties, takes a new form.

That which is not to be expropriated is no longer the labourer
working for himself, but the capitalist exploiting many labourers.
60 This expropriation is accomplished by the action of the immanent
laws of capitalistic production itself, by the centralisation of capital.
One capitalist always kills many. . . .

Along with the constantly diminishing number of the magnates
of capital, who usurp and monopolise all advantages of this process
65 of transformation, grows the mass of misery, oppressions, slavery,
degradation, exploitation, but with this too grows the revolt of the
working class, always increasing in numbers, and disciplined,
united, organised by the very mechanism of the process of capitalist
production itself. The monopoly of capital becomes a fetter upon
70 the mode of production, which has sprung up and flourished along
with, and under it. Centralisations of the means of production and
socialisation of labour at last reach a point where they become
incompatible with their capitalist integument. This integument is
burst asunder. The knell of capitalist private property sounds. The
75 expropriators are expropriated. . . .

Karl Marx, *Capital*, vol I (Chicago, Charles Kerr, 1906) ch.
22

(e) *Private property*

You are horrified at our intending to do away with private property.
But in your existing society, private property is already done away
with for nine-tenths of the population; its existence for the few is
solely due to its non-existence in the hands of those nine-tenths.
80 You reproach us, therefore, with intending to do away with a form
of property the necessary condition for whose existence is the non-
existence of any property for the immense majority of society.

In one word, you reproach us with intending to do away with
your property. Precisely so; that is just what we intend.
85 . . . By freedom is meant, under the present bourgeois conditions
of production, free trade, free selling and buying.

But if selling and buying disappears, free selling and buying
disappears also. This talk about free selling and buying, and all
other 'brave words' of our bourgeoisie about freedom in general,
90 have a meaning, if any, only in contrast with restricted selling and
buying and selling of the bourgeois conditions of production, and
of the bourgeoisie itself.

. . . Communism deprives no man of the power to appropriate
the products of society; all that it does is to deprive him of the power
95 to subjugate the labour of others by means of such appropriation.

Marx and Engels, op cit, pp 98–9

(f) The immediate tasks of a communist government

The first step in the revolution by the working class, is to raise the proletariat to the position of ruling class, to win the battle of democracy.

100 The proletariat will use its political supremacy to wrest, by degrees, all capital from the bourgeoisie, to centralize all instruments of production in the hands of the State, i.e., of the proletariat organized as the ruling class; and to increase the total of productive forces as rapidly as possible.

. . .

These measures will of course be different in different countries.
105 Nevertheless, in the most advanced countries, the following will be pretty generally applicable:

   1. Abolition of property in land and application of all rents of land to public purposes.
   2. A heavy progressive or graduated income tax.
110   3. Confiscation of the property of all emigrants and rebels.
   4. Abolition of all right of inheritance.
   5. Centralization of credit in the hands of the State, by means of a national bank with State capital and an exclusive monopoly.
115   6. Centralization of the means of communication and transport in the hands of the State.
   7. Extension of factories and instruments of production owned by the State; the bringing into cultivation of wastelands, and the improvement of the soil generally in accordance with a
120   common plan.
   8. Equal liabilities of all to labour. Establishment of industrial armies, especially for agriculture.
   9. Combination of agriculture with manufacturing industries; gradual abolition of the distinction between town and
125   country, by a more equable distribution of the population over the country.
  10. Free education for all children in public schools. Abolition of children's factory labour in its present form. Combination of education with industrial production, &c., &c.
130 When, in the course of development, class distinctions have disappeared, and all production has been concentrated in the whole nation, the public power will lose its political character. Political power, properly so called, is merely the organized power of one class for oppressing another. If the proletariat during its contest
135 with the bourgeoisie is compelled, by the force of circumstances, to organize itself as a class, if by means of a revolution, it makes itself the ruling class, and, as such, sweeps away by force the old conditions of production, then it will, along with these conditions, have swept away the conditions for the existence of class antago-
140 nisms and of classes generally, and will thereby have abolished its own supremacy as a class.

In place of the old bourgeois society, with its classes and class antagonisms, we shall have an association, in which the free development of each is the condition for the free development of
145 all.

Ibid, pp 104–5

Questions

a In extract (c) what exactly is the class struggle?
b Give examples of occupations held by each of the three classes.
c According to extract (d), how does a labourer become a proletarian and what is the difference between the two positions?
d How does capitalism lead to the revolt of the workers?
e Why is private property unfair, according to extract (e)?
f In extract (f), when and how will class distinctions and the organised state disappear?
★ g How radical are the ten· measures listed here? Which have been applied in present day Britain?
★ h How precise was Marx on how, where and when a proletariat revolution would break out?

2 Russia

(a) Industrial development

Before 1861, 2,177 enterprises were initiated; between 1861 and 1870, 1,285; between 1871 and 1880, 2,100; between 1881 and 1890, 3,030; between 1891 and 1900, 5,788. So 40 per cent. of the establishments mentioned in the list cited were founded during the
5 latter portion of the nineteenth century. In spite of its youth, or perhaps for that very reason, the industrial capitalism of Russia gives evidence of stupendous energy and a great faculty of growth. . . .
'While the production of cast metal increased, between 1890–1900, by 58 per cent. in France, 13 per cent. in Great Britain, 76
10 per cent. in the United States, and 61 per cent. in Germany, in Russia it increased by 220 per cent. The production of iron and steel during the same ten years increased by 42 per cent. in France, 50 per cent. in the United States, 91 per cent. in Germany, and 196 per cent. in Russia. Thus the increase in production of Russia
15 in this industrial sphere has sensibly exceeded that of the world, and has enormously exceeded that of each capitalist country considered separately' (A. Finn-Yenotaevsky, *Industrial Capitalism in Russia during the last Ten Years of the Nineteenth Century*). Such is the statement of a Russian economist. The reader must not forget

20   that the social and political conditions beside which Russian capitalism has had to develop have been far from favourable to the latter. If the juridical and political formation of the life of the Russian people could be so reformed as to give the productive forces of the country entire liberty, we might count upon a still

25   more rapid development of Russian capitalism. With its abundance of natural wealth, Russia would become a dangerous rival even of the most advanced nations.

      One of the peculiarities of Russian capitalism is the part which foreign capital has played in its development. Some branches of

30   Russian industry – mining and metallurgy – exist very largely by means of foreign capital. This participation of European money in the economic life of Russia has had two results. In the first place, it has bound Russian capitalism closely to European capitalism. Everything that happens in Russia has an interest for the capitalist

35   world of France, England, and Belgium which is not only theoretical, but material; for enormous quantities of gold are invested by these countries in the industrial undertakings of Russia. Still greater are the sums which enter Russia from abroad in the form of State loans. These loans, concluded not at home but abroad, have earned

40   and do still earn a steady profit, not for the Russian middle classes, but for foreign capitalists. Finally, we find that the development of foreign capital in Russia is detrimental to the development of Russian capital. The cause of this phenomenon is the political weakness of the Russian middle classes. The autocracy, with the

45   aid of European capital, has not only succeeded in making itself independent of the middle classes, but it refuses to allow the latter to acquire political power.

      Gregor Alexinsky, *Modern Russia* (1913) pp 102–3

(b) *Another viewpoint*

    Arising late, Russian industry did not repeat the development of the advanced countries, but inserted itself into this development,

50   adapting their latest achievements to its own backwardness. Just as the economic evolution of Russia as a whole skipped over the epoch of craft-guilds and manufacture, so also the separate branches of industry made a series of special leaps over technical productive stages that had been measured in the West by decades. Thanks to

55   this, Russian industry developed at certain periods with extraordinary speed. Between the first revolution and the war, industrial production in Russia approximately doubled.

    . . .

    The basic criterion of the economic level of a nation is the productivity of labour, which in its turn depends upon the relative

60   weight of the industries in the general economy of the country.

On the eve of the war, when tzarist Russia had attained the highest
point of its prosperity, the national income per capita was 8 to 10
times less than in the United States – a fact which is not surprising
when you consider that $\frac{4}{5}$ of the self-supporting population of
Russia was occupied with agriculture, while in the United States,
for every one engaged in agriculture, $2\frac{1}{2}$ were engaged in industry.
65   We must add that for every one hundred squared kilometers of
land, Russia had, on the eve of the war, 0.4 kilometers of railroads,
Germany 11.7, Austria–Hungary 7. Other comparative coefficients
are of the same type.

Leon Trotsky, *The History of the Russian Revolution* (New
York, 1980) p 9

Questions

a   According to extract (a), which period in Russia's history has
      seen the greatest industrial growth?
b   Explain the comment 'social and political conditions beside
      which Russian capitalism has had to develop have been far from
      favourable to the latter' (lines 20–2).
c   In extract (b) Trotsky agrees that Russian industry has expanded
      greatly. What weaknesses does he find in the economy?
d   Why would the evidence of both these extracts be encouraging
      to the communists in Russia at this time?

(c) Tsarist law and order

The application of the death penalty has been terribly frequent
during the last few years. M. Gruzenberg, the well-known jurist
of St. Petersburg, has published the following figures in an article
in the juridical review Pravo (The Law):
5   'In 1908, during the intensely critical period of the third Duma,
the period of pacification by the Government, 7,016 civilians were
delivered over to the military tribunals by virtue of emergency
laws. Of these, 1,340 were condemned to death. In one single year
more men were executed than during the preceding thirty-three
10   years of the history of these courts, and one and a half times more
than during the so-called revolutionary period (1905–7).'
      Do not forget that these figures relate only to capital punishment
sanctioned by 'justice'. A greater number of victims of the reaction
perished without trial: in two years (1905–6), during the 'stifling
15   of the revolutionary movement,' 26,000 persons were killed by the
army and the police, while 31,000 were wounded. But these figures
do not include the victims of the notorious 'punitive detachments.'
These, in the Baltic provinces alone, killed 1,500 to 2,000 of the
inhabitants. Add to these 37,000 victims of the pogroms (1905–10)

20 and you will realize what horrible sacrifices the Russian people has
offered upon the altar of liberty!

The number of those detained in prison has increased incredibly:
in 1897 it was 77,000: in 1909 it was 181,000. These unfortunates
consist principally of political 'criminals.' As for the number of
25 those deported to the north of European Russia or Siberia, it is so
great that it cannot be established.

. . .

I will spare my readers a description of the horrors committed
in the depths of the Russian prisons and in Siberia. The prison
administration treats those detained on political grounds with the
30 utmost brutality, employing the worst forms of torture and corporal
punishment, and the walls of prisons often witness frightful
tragedies and wholesale suicides, since suicide is the sole means of
protest left to the prisoner.

Alexinsky, op cit, pp 94–5

(d) Political life

Work in secret, illegal organizations had created a special type,
35 the 'professional revolutionary,' with no occupation in life but
revolution. He was in his own way a magnificent type of the
wandering apostle of socialism and of the knight errant protector of
the oppressed and punisher of ravishers. Prison was his university,
where at forced leisure he feverishly supplemented his intellectual
40 baggage; the repressions and cruelties of the jailors were a test of
endurance and firmness of spirit; escapes were episodes; conspiracy
and disguise a habit; hiding from detectives a sport; propaganda
and agitation an indispensable necessity. At the London congress
of the Social Democratic party (338 present) a questionnaire among
45 the participants showed that they had spent 597 years under the
official supervision of the police, in prison, exile and galley labour,
had been arraigned 710 times and effected 201 escapes; yet their
average age was twenty-eight. An even greater record of persecution
was typical of the Social Revolutionaries. At their London conferen-
50 ces with 61 present, they totalled 121 years of exile, 104 years of
prison, 88 years of galley labour, 228 police raids, 146 arrests. In
the secret organizations the professional revolutionaries set the tone.
The members of the scattered system of local committees, built up
on a more or less strict centralization, looked to them, patterned
55 themselves after them.

Victor Chernov, *The Great Russian Revolution* (New York,
1966) pp 98–9

a   What criticisms are implicit in the description of Russian law
    and order in extract (c)?
b   According to extract (d), how did conditions in Russia affect
    political parties there?
★
c   Why was the Russian government so repressive?

3   Russian Political Parties

(a) A British view

Long before I had mastered enough Russian to take part in the
general conversation, I suspected that the Ertels were bitterly
opposed to the Tsarist form of Government, and that their
sympathies were with the Cadets and Social-revolutionaries. As my
5   Russian improved (in four months I could speak with considerable
fluency), my suspicions were confirmed, and the knowledge that I
was living in an anti-Tsarist stronghold gave a new thrill to my
life and an added zest to my Russian studies. The thrill became
almost a fear when one day over evening tea I was introduced to a
10 woman whose husband had been shot during the 1905 revolution.
I mentioned this episode to Montgomery Grove, who shook his
head gravely and warned me to be careful. Nothing untoward,
however, happened to me through this association. Later I was to
realise that all the Moscow 'intelligenzia' shared the Ertelian view.
15   The Ertels, in fact, were typical representatives of the intelligenzia. When at ten o'clock every evening they assembled round the
samovar, they would sometimes sit far into the night discussing
how to make the world safe by revolution.
        But when the morning of action came they were fast asleep in
20 bed. It was very harmless, very hopeless, and very Russian. But
for the war and the antiquated inefficiency of the Russian military
organisation, the Tsar would still be on his throne.
        Let me create no false impression. My Russian friends were not
obsessed by revolution. Politics, in fact, were reserved for special
25 occasions such as unhappy political anniversaries or some outrage-
ous political sentence in the Russian courts. At other times the
conversation was stimulating and instructive.
        R. H. Bruce Lockhart, *Memoirs of a British Agent* (1974)
        pp 65–6

(b) Cadets

Constitutional–Democrats – members of the Constitutional–Democratic Party, the principal party of the Russian liberal–monarchist

30   bourgeoisie, founded in October 1905. It consisted of representatives of the bourgeoisie, landowner and bourgeois intellectuals;
subsequently it became a party of the imperialist bourgeoisie.

    To deceive the working people the Cadets assumed the false
name of 'the party of the people's freedom' but actually they never
35   went beyond the demand for a constitutional monarchy.

          V. I. Lenin, *The Immediate Tasks of the Soviet Government*
(Moscow, 1970) p 48

(c) Cadets

Cadets. So-called from the initials of its name, Constitutional
Democrats. Its official name is 'Party of the People's Freedom'.
Under the Tsar composed of Liberals from the propertied classes,
the Cadets were the great party of political reform, roughly
40   corresponding to the Progressive Party in America. . . . As the
revolution became more and more a social economic revolution,
the Cadets grew more and more conservative. Its representatives
in this book are: Milyukov, Vinaver, Shatsky.

          John Reed, *Ten Days that Shook the World* (1982) p 19

Questions

a   In extract (a) what is the author's attitude towards the intelligentsia in Russia?
b   What does the final sentence mean: 'At other times the conversation was stimulating and instructive' (lines 26–7)?
c   Compare the two definitions in extracts (b) and (c). Are they
in favour of the party or not?

(d) Background to the Social Revolutionaries

When the Social-Revolutionaries began their work, Russia had but
little industry, and an urban proletariat practically did not exist in
the country. Thus they became, in consequence both of their
theories and of the medium with which they had to deal, primarily
5   a peasant party, making appeal to the rural population, championing
its needs, and striving to enlighten its mind. That is why the
peasants were almost solid on their side during the first months of
the Revolution. Its indigenous character, and its limitation to
conditions which existed only in Russia, helped to make Social-
10   Revolutionism 'national,' or patriotic. It was not easy to form close
international connections on the basis of a doctrine which was quite
inapplicable to other countries. This accounts for the stalwart

fidelity of all the Social-Revolutionaries of the old school to the cause of the Allies in the War.

15   Another of the distinguishing characteristics of the Social-Revolutionaries was that they deliberately adopted and practised political terrorism, and it was they who carried out those assassinations of members of the reigning family, Cabinet Ministers and high officials, which from time to time startled and shocked the world.
20   This is not the place to discuss the morality and justifiability of murder as a political weapon. It is a complicated question, which cannot be settled by English standards. The standpoint of the Social-Revolutionaries was that the system by which Russia was governed was an iniquitous one, involving untold injustice and
25   misery to innocent people, that those in high office were responsible for it, and that menace to their lives was the only means of exercising pressure on them. On the whole, terrorism seems to have had effects exactly contrary to those anticipated from it, and to have aggravated the evils it was intended to cure. It should not
30   be forgotten, however, that a very large proportion of those who practised it were members of aristocratic and wealthy families, who voluntarily surrendered positions of privilege and ease, and sacrificed their lives or liberty for a cause from which they personally had everything to lose and nothing to gain.
E. H. Wilcox, *Russia's Ruin* (1919) pp 156–7

(e) *Definition*

35   Socialist-Revolutionaries (S.R.s) – a petty-bourgeois party in Russia which came into being at the end of 1901 and the beginning of 1902 as a result of the merger of various Narodnik groups and circles. The S.R.s did not see the class distinctions between the proletariat and the petty proprietors, glossed over the class
40   stratification and contradictions within the peasantry and denied the proletariat's leading role in the revolution. The S.R.s called themselves socialists but their socialism was a far cry from truly scientific socialism. It was petty-bourgeois socialism based on equalitarian land tenure, so-called socialisation of the land, which
45   would only facilitate the development of capitalism.
Lenin, *The Immediate Tasks*, op cit, p 48

(f) *Social Revolutionaries: Beliefs*

The Social Revolutionaries maintained that a bourgeois revolution, which would affect the form of government only, without touching social structure and property relationships, and open the way to capitalist hegemony in every field of economic life, was impossible

50 in Russia. There was no bourgeoisie fit for leadership in a revolution
of that type, since the Russian bourgeoisie was, by all its antecedents,
certain to be an integral part of the alliance of reactionary forces
led by the Tsarist government. On the other hand, the Russian
Revolutionaries realized that Russia's toiling masses lacked the
55 a radical blow to the institution of private property. The Social
Revolutionaries realised that Russia's toiling masses lacked the
maturity, and the training in economic self-government, in cooperative association, and in management of autonomous labour organisations requisite to the establishment of a socialist society. Yet
60 instead of drawing a metaphysical line of demarcations between
capitalism and socialism, they visualised a long transition period of
'labourism'.
. . .
The new order would not be socialism, but the building of a
new social-labour legislation within the framework of a money
65 economy. It would represent the gradual development of collective
forms of economic activity or of control over economy at the
expense of purely individual economy. . . .
It would include the evolution of cooperation, speeded up by
the support of the state, the development of municipal and
70 government enterprise, the growth of a system of factory constitu-
tionalism, with the creation of a self-administering industrial
republic as its final term.
Chernov, op cit, pp 113–14

Questions

a What were the beliefs of the Social Revolutionaries according
to extract (d)?
b How does the writer of extract (d) attempt to excuse the policy
of political terrorism?
c In what ways is extract (e) antagonistic towards the Social
Revolutionaries?
d In extract (f) what is the Social Revolutionaries attitude towards
the bourgeoisie and socialism?

4 Russian Communism

(a) *The Proletarian Revolution*

The opportunists of the Second International have a number of
theoretical dogmas to which they always revert as their starting
point. Let us take a few of these.
First dogma: concerning the conditions for the seizure of power
5 by the proletariat. The opportunists assert that the proletariat

cannot and ought not to take power unless it constitutes a majority in the country. No proofs are brought forward, for there are no proofs, either theoretical or practical, that can bear out this absurd thesis. Let us assume that this is so, Lenin replies to the gentlemen
10 of the Second International; but suppose a historical situation has arisen (a war, an agrarian crisis, etc.) in which the proletariat, constituting a minority of the population, has an opportunity to rally around itself the vast majority of the labouring masses; why should it not take power then?

Speeches in *Pravda*, April/May 1924 reprinted in J. V. Stalin, *The Foundations of Leninism* (Peking, 1970) p 15

(b) *The permanent revolution*

15 It is possible for the workers to come into power in economically backward countries sooner than in advanced countries. In 1871 the workers took power in their hands in petty bourgeois Paris – true it lasted for only two months, but in highly developed capitalist England or the United States the workers have never held power
20 for a single hour. To imagine that the dictatorship of the proletariat is in some way automatically dependent on the technical development of a country is reducing 'economic' materialism to absurdity. This point of view has nothing in common with Marxism.

In our view the Russian Revolution will create conditions in
25 which power will pass into the hands of the workers – and in the event of the victory of the revolution, it must pass into the hands of the workers – before the bourgeoisie is able to develop their ability to govern.

Leon Trotsky, *A Review and some Perspectives* (Moscow, 1921) p 36

(c) *A commentary on Lenin*

The Russian bourgeoisie was antidemocratic, greedy for compro-
30 mise with Tsarism because of its own hatred for the labour movement. Therefore, the bourgeois revolution had to be carried out against the bourgeoisie. The working class must carry out that revolution for it. The unreliability of the bourgeoisie as an ally it must remedy by alliance with the peasantry. 'The bourgeois
35 revolution, achieved by the proletariat and peasantry despite the instability of the bourgeoisie – that is a main thesis of Bolshevist tactics,' Lenin proclaimed at that time. In case of extremity, an allied dictatorship of the proletariat and peasantry was possible, but its mission would be merely to squeeze from the bourgeois-

40 democratic revolution all its revolutionary consequences, and, in
no case, to advance to the socialist revolution.

The Mensheviks refused to follow Lenin on this path; they
regarded it as a political adventure. From their point of view, a
socialist party could suffer no worse misfortune than to achieve
45 power at a time when the country was not prepared for socialism.

Chernov, op cit, pp 112–13

(d) Social Democrats

In the beginning Social Democracy, before it divided into Bolsheviks and Mensheviks, derived from prewar orthodox Marxism.
It considered that Russia's historial evolution would, by and large,
follow the well-beaten track of the Western European countries.
50 This was the path of capitalist development. It would be longer
for Russia, a poor agrarian country, whose industrialization was
impeded by the presence of powerful international competitors; yet
Russia had to be not only industrialized, but transformed from a
poor capitalist country into a wealthy one. The mission of Russia's
55 approaching revolution, like the first revolutions of other European
states, was merely to clear the way for her capitalist evolution, to
free her of all pre-capitalist survivals, of servile, forced labour, of
the political absolutism which fettered the initiative and activity of
her population. With the fall of autocracy the rule of the bourgeoisie
60 would begin; hence the leading role in eliminating absolutism must
fall to the bourgeoisie. The proletariat, as the historic heir to
the bourgeoisie, must arm itself with patience and first aid the
bourgeoisie, the historic heir of absolutism, to claim its inheritance.
Thus, the role of the proletariat was (1) to support the liberal
65 bourgeoisie against absolutism, (2) to urge it forward in eliminating
autocracy completely, instead of patching up some shoddy compromise, (3) in return for its support to gain from the bourgeois
revolution full liberty for its own further organization, both political
and trade union, full right to participate in deciding matters of state
70 and in creating legislation which would give the proletariat more
and more influence in the factory.

Such was the original classical view of Social Democracy regarding the coming revolution and the role of the proletariat.

Ibid, pp 110–11

(e) Definition

Mensheviks – supporters of the petty-bourgeois trend in Russian
75 Social-Democracy, vehicles of bourgeois influence among the
workers. The name (meaning members of the minority) dates from

the Second Congress of the R.S.D.L.P. in August 1903: in the elections to the central bodies of the Party, held at the end of the Congress, they were in the minority, while the revolutionary Social-
80 Democrats, headed by Lenin, constituted the majority ('Bolsheviks' means members of the majority). The Mensheviks urged for an agreement between the proletariat and the bourgeoisie and pursued an opportunist policy in the working-class movement.

Lenin, *The Immediate Tasks*, op cit, pp 47–8

(f) Definition

(a) Mensheviki. This party includes all shades of socialists who
85 believe that society must progress by natural evolution towards socialism, and that the working class must conquer political power first. Also a nationalistic party. This was the party of the socialist intellectuals, which means: all the means of education having been in the hands of the propertied classes, the intellectuals instinctively
90 reacted to their training, and took the side of the propertied classes. Among their represenatatives in this book are: Dan, Lieber, Tseretelly.

Reed, op cit, p 20

(g) The professional revolutionary

The organization of a revolutionary Social-Democratic party must inevitably be of a different kind from an organization of workers
95 for such a struggle. An organization of workers must be first a trade organization; secondly, it must be as broad as possible; thirdly, it must be as little secret as possible (here and farther on I speak, of course, only with autocratic Russia in mind). An organization of revolutionaries, on the contrary, must embrace primarily and
100 chiefly people whose profession consists of revolutionary activity (it is because of this that I speak of an organization of revolutionaries, having in mind revolutionary Social Democrats). In the face of this common feature of the members of such an organisation, any distinction between workers and intellectuals must be completely
105 obliterated, not to speak of differences between separate professions and trades. This organization must inevitably be not very wide and as secret as possible . . . professional revolutionaries, irrespective of whether they develop out of students or out of workers. And now I maintain: (1) that no revolutionary movement can be durable
110 without a stable organization of leaders which preserves continuity; (2) that the broader the mass which is spontaneously drawn into the struggle, which forms the basis of the movement and participates in it, the more urgent is the necessity for such an organization, and

the more durable this organization must be (because the broader
115 the mass, the easier it is for any demagogue to attract the backward
sections of the mass); (3) that such an organization must consist
mainly of people who are professionally engaged in revolutionary
activities: (4) that, in an autocratic country, the more we narrow
the membership of such an organization, restricting it only to those
120 who are professionally engaged in revolutionary activities and have
received a professional training in the art of struggle against the
political police, the more difficult will it be to 'catch' such an
organization; and (5) the wider will be the category of people, both
from the working class and from other classes of society, who will
125 have an opportunity of participating in the movement and actively
working in it.

V. I. Lenin, *What is to be done?* (1970) pp 156, 159, 169–71

Questions

a   According to extract (a), in what ways might the proletariat
seize power when in a minority?

b   What is the argument regarding the proletariat revolution
outlined in extract (b)? How does it differ from extract (a)?

c   Compare extract (c) with the previous two extracts.

d   Extract (d) was written by a critic of the Bolsheviks. How do
his ideas vary from those in extracts (a) and (b)?

e   Are extracts (e) and (f) in favour of or antagonistic towards
the Mensheviks?

f   In extract (g), what was a professional revolutionary and why
was he needed?

★ g   Draw up a table and compare the attitudes of the Bolsheviks
and Mensheviks towards:

    (i) the party leadership;
    (ii) relations with other parties;
    (iii) the role of the proletariat in the bourgeois revolution.

★ h   Compare the attitudes of the Bolsheviks and Social Revolutionaries to:

    (i) political assassination;
    (ii) peasant ownership of land.

II   *The February Revolution*

Introduction

Marx claimed that two circumstances might precipitate a revolution: a major war or a serious economic depression. Both proved to be important in Russia in the First World War as the country failed to cope with the war's demands for, as Trotsky pointed out, if Russia could not defeat a small country like Japan in 1905 it should come as no surprise that it would have even more difficulty in a major war with both Germany and Austria.

The outbreak of war in 1914 was greeted in Russia, as in other countries, with great public enthusiasm. For a brief period the tsar became popular again but the honeymoon did not last for long. Ill-equipped and badly led, the Russian army lurched from disaster to disaster. Industry was insufficient to meet war demands. Agriculture was similarly inadequate. The biggest landlords with the most efficient farms saw their peasants conscripted into the armies. The independent peasant farmer who barely produced enough food for his own family saw no reason to work any harder and produce more. He had no use for the extra money, which was largely worthless as the government frantically printed more notes in a foolish attempt to pay their bills; and there was no chance of acquiring consumer goods when all factories were now geared to war production. As a result, food production slumped, the cities starved. The first serious bread riots broke out in Petrograd in late February 1917.

If they began as aimless riots, it was not long before the government began to take the blame for this desperate state of affairs. The tsar had taken personal command of the armed forces early in the war, a move which did nothing to improve Russia's ability to fight but did lead Nicholas to be blamed personally for the country's continuing poor performance. It also took him away from Petrograd and from a true understanding of political life in the capital. Everyday government fell into the hands of Empress Alexandra, hated for being a German, and her chief confidant, the debauched and politically inexperienced Rasputin. This 'Holy Man' was eventually murdered by a number of nobles in a desperate attempt to re-establish the popularity of the government.

When the February Revolution proved that this move was too late, moderates decided on a bigger sacrifice, Tsar Nicholas II himself. The initial plan was merely to replace him with a more efficient ruler, perhaps his brother. Typically, Nicholas accepted this plan with little protest; but no one would accept the vacant position. More by accident than design, Russia went from absolute monarchy to no monarchy overnight.

1 First World War

(a) The 1905 revolution

The events of 1905 were a prologue to the two revolutions of 1917, that of February and that of October. In the prologue all the elements of the drama were included, but not carried through. The Russo-Japanese war had made tzarism totter. Against the back-
5   ground of a mass movement the liberal bourgeoisie had frightened the monarchy with its opposition. The workers had organized independently of the bourgeoisie, and in opposition to it, in soviets, a form of organization then first called into being. Peasant uprisings to seize the land occurred throughout vast stretches of the country.
10 Not only the peasants, but also the revolutionary parts of the army tended toward the soviets, which at the moment of highest tension openly disputed the power with the monarchy. However, all the revolutionary forces were then going into action for the first time, lacking experience and confidence. The liberals demonstratively
15 backed away from the revolution exactly at the moment when it became clear that to shake tzarism would not be enough, it must be overthrown. This sharp break of the bourgeoisie with the people, in which the bourgeoisie carried with it considerable circles of the democratic intelligentsia, made it easier for the monarchy to
20 differentiate within the army, separating out the loyal units, and to make a bloody settlement with the workers and peasants. Although with a few broken ribs, tzarism came out of the experience of 1905 alive and strong enough.

Trotsky, *The Russian Revolution*, op cit, pp 12–13

(b) War fever

Monday, August 17th – The arrival of Their Majesties at Moscow
25 has been one of the most impressive and moving sights I have ever seen in my life.

After the customary reception at the station we went in a long file of carriages towards the Kremlin. An enormous crowd had collected in the squares and in the streets, climbed on the roofs of
30 the shops, into the branches of trees. They swarmed in the shop

windows and filled the balconies and windows of the houses. While
all the bells of the churches were ringing as if they would never
stop, from those thousands of throats poured that wonderful
Russian National Anthem, so overwhelming with its religious
35 grandeur and pent emotion, in which the faith of a whole race is
embodied:

'God save the Czar!
Mighty and powerful, let him reign for our glory.
For the confusion of our enemies, the orthodox Czar.
40 God save the Czar!'

On the steps of the churches, through the great doorways of which
one could see the light of the candles burning before the reliquaries,
the priests in vestments, and holding their great crucifixes in both
hands, blessed the Czar as he passed. The hymn stopped, and then
45 began again, rising like a prayer with a mighty and majestic rhythm:

'God save the Czar!'
Pierre Gilliard, *13 Years at the Russian Court* (1972) p 112

(c) *Trotsky on the war*

Like revolution, war forces life, from top to bottom, away from
the beaten track. But revolution directs its blows against the
established power. War, on the contrary, at first strengthens the
50 state power which, in the chaos engendered by war, appears to be
the only firm support – and then undermines it. Hopes of strong
social and national movements, whether it be in Prague or in
Trieste, in Warsaw or Tiflis, are utterly groundless at the outset of
a war. In September 1914 I wrote to Russia: 'The mobilization and
55 declaration of war have veritably swept off the face of the earth all
the national and social contradictions in the country. But this is
only a political delay, a sort of political moratorium. The notes
have been extended to a new date, but they will have to be paid.'
In these censored lines, I referred, of course, not only to Austria–
60 Hungary, but to Russia as well – in fact, to Russia most of all.
Leon Trotsky, *My Life* (1971) p 241

(d) *Liberals and the war*

The war of 1914 was quite rightly greeted by the leaders of the
Russian bourgeoisie as their war. In a solemn session of the State
Duma on July 26, 1914, the president of the Kadet faction
announced: 'We will make no conditions or demands. We will
65 simply throw in the scales, our firm determination to conquer the
enemy.' In Russia, too, national unity became the official doctrine.
Trotsky, *The Russian Revolution*, op cit, p 23

   a   Why, according to extract (a), did the 1905 revolution fail?
   b   What impression of the start of the war is given in extract (b)?
   c   In extract (c), what are the differences between war and revolution?
   d   Extract (d) is taken from Trotsky's autobiography. Why do you think he wrote this section?
★   *e*   Why was there war fever in Russia and the other main powers at the beginning of the war?

(e) The Russian army

The semi-annulment of serfdom and the introduction of universal military service had modernized the army only as far as it had the country – that is, it introduced into the army all the contradictions proper to a nation which still has its bourgeois revolution to
5   accomplish. It is true that the tzar's army was constructed and armed upon Western models; but this was more form than essence. There was no correspondence between the cultural level of the peasant–soldier and modern military technique. In the commanding staff, the ignorance, light-mindedness, and thievery of the ruling
10 classes found their expression. Industry and transport continually revealed their bankruptcy before the concentrated demands of wartime. Although appropriately armed, as it seemed, on the first day of the war, the troops soon turned out to have neither weapons nor even shoes. In the Russo-Japanese war the tzarist army had
15 shown what it was worth. In the epoch of counter-revolution the monarchy, with the aid of the Duma, had filled up the military stores and put many new patches on the army, especially upon its reputation for invincibility. In 1914 came a new and far heavier test.
            Ibid, pp. 17–18

(f) The outlook of the Russian army, January 1917

20 When this mass is at last demobilised and poured out over the country, it will wash away old landmarks and destroy dykes which have kept back the flood. All will join in one general demand: that the government should answer for bringing the country to the state it is in. To what extent the Government is really responsible will
25 not concern them. Everyone agrees that there will be a revolution. On this occasion the Army will be on the side of the people. . . .
     Among the better class of officers I note a great change of late. It daily grows greater and franker, daily more freely expressed. That is their attitude towards the Emperor. From time immemorial
30 they have abused the Government. In the last year I have noticed a

new and sinister trend of feeling towards the Emperor. One by
one they have fallen away from him, louder and louder they declare
the existing state of affairs to be impossible.

35   They condemn the Emperor as being weak and vacillating, ruled
by the Empress and keeping in office Ministers not only utterly
incompetent, but with pro-German tendencies.

. . . The war has brought out all that is worst in Russia, not the
best. The enthusiasm that at one time was felt, evaporated as the
war dragged on, leaving only apathy as regards the war and a
40   feverish thirst for money. The opinion of the Army is that those
left in the towns have no thought for the war, but only for money
making.

. . . I have omitted to say that no officer or private soldier has a
good word to say for the Empress. All place her at the head of the
45   pro-German party, all genuinely hate her.

Public Record Office: FO 371 3003 (A report on the Russian
Army)

(g) War weariness

The revolutionary elements, scattered at first, were drowned in the
army almost without a trace, but with the growth of the general
discontent they rose to the surface. The sending of striking workers
to the front as a punishment increased the ranks of the agitators
50   and the retreat gave them a favourable audience. 'The Army, in
the rear and especially at the front,' reports a secret service agent,
'is full of elements of which some are capable of becoming active
forces of insurrection, and others may merely refuse to engage in
punitive activities.' The Gendarme Administration of the Petrograd
55   province declares in October 1916, on the basis of a report made
by a representative of the Land Union, that 'the mood in the army
is alarming, the relation between officers and soldiers is extremely
tense, even everywhere by the thousands. Everyone who comes
near the army must carry away a complete and convincing
60   impression of the utter moral disintegration of the troops.' Out of
caution the report adds that although much in these communications
seems hardly probable, nevertheless it must be believed, since many
physicians returning from the active army have made reports to
the same effect. The mood of the rear corresponded to that of the
65   front. At a conference of the Kadet party in October 1916, a
majority of the delegates remarked upon the apathy and lack of
faith in the victorious outcome of the war 'in all layers of the
population, but especially in the villages and among the city poor.'
On October 30, 1916, the director of the Police Department wrote,
70   in a summary of his report, of 'the weariness of war to be observed
everywhere, and the longing for a swift peace, regardless of the

conditions upon which it is concluded.' In a few months all these gentlemen – deputies, police, generals and land representatives, physicians and former gendarmes – will nevertheless assert that the
75 revolution killed patriotism in the army, and that the Bolsheviks snatched a sure victory out of their hands.

Trotsky, *The Russian Revolution*, op cit, p 56

(h) Another version

The report of the director of the Petrograd Gendarme Department for October, 1916, contained extracts from a report prepared by them for the proposed Moscow conferences of the Workers' Groups
80 of the War Industries Committees:

'The war is daily adding tens of thousands to the opponents of war and militarism. . . . The discord of party programs, lack of proper organization among the several classes of the population, impossibility of carrying on propaganda, etc., compel the Social
85 Revolutionaries to view things differently from the Social Democrats and other Left-wing parties: in Russia a revolution on the 1905 model is impossible at present, but a combined revolution by the military and working-class masses is more than possible.

The success of the propaganda of the Social Revolutionaries in
90 the army, concerning which new data are arriving daily, leads us to expect that the revolution will be begun by those soldiers formed from yesterday's workers and by those workers who are subjected to the galley-like rule of the militaristic police state, and driven to work by bullets and bayonets.'
95 The director of the Gendarme Department pessimistically agreed that 'certain facts, such as success in spreading pacifism among the soldiers and the militarized workers, growth of general discontent with the high cost of living and lack of food . . . are true, and the Social Revolutionary agitators correctly realize that the present
100 moment is most favourable for harrowing the soil to receive revolutionary ideas and Utopias.'

Chernov, op cit, p 100

Questions

a   According to extract (e), what were the weaknesses of the Russian army?

b   What conclusions does the author of extract (f) reach about the Russian army?

c   According to this extract, why might the army dislike the civilians in the towns?

★ d   Why was the Empress accused of leading a pro-German group?

e In extract (g), explain the final sentence 'In a few months . . . out of their hands' (lines 72–6).

★ *f* Both extracts (g) and (h) refer to a report by the Petrograd Gendarme Department. Why do these two writers use different extracts from the same report?

2 The February Revolution

(a) Strikes

The 23rd of February was International Woman's Day. The social-democratic circles had intended to mark this day in a general manner: by meetings, speeches, leaflets. It had not occurred to anyone that it might become the first day of the revolution. Not a
5   single organization called for strikes on that day. What is more, even a Bolshevik organization, and a most militant one – the Vyborg borough-committee, all workers – was opposing strikes. . . .

On the following morning, however, in spite of all directives, the women textile workers in several factories went on strike, and
10 sent delegates to the metal workers with an appeal for support. . . .

The overgrown bread-lines had provided the last stimulus. About 90,000 workers, men and women, were on strike that day. The fighting mood expressed itself in demonstrations, meetings, encounters with the police. The movement began in the Vyborg
15 district with its large industrial establishments; thence it crossed over to the Petersburg side. There were no strikes or demonstrations elsewhere, according to the testimony of the secret police. On that day detachments of troops were called in to assist the police – evidently not many of them – but there were no encounters with
20 them. A mass of women, not all of them workers, flocked to the municipal duma demanding bread. It was like demanding milk from a he-goat. Red banners appeared in different parts of the city, and inscriptions on them showed that the workers wanted bread, but neither autocracy nor war. Woman's Day passed successfully,
25 with enthusiasm and without victims. But what it concealed in itself, no one had guessed even by nightfall.

Trotsky, *My Life*, op cit, pp 101–2

(b) Rumours

On Saturday 25th Petersburg seethed in an atmosphere of extraordinary events from the morning on. The streets, even where there was no concentration of people, were a picture of extreme
30 excitement. I was reminded of the 1905 Moscow insurrection. The entire civil population felt itself to be in one camp united against the enemy – the police and the military. Strangers passing by

conversed with each other, asking questions and talking about the
news, about clashes with and the diversionary movements of the
35 enemy.
   But something else was noticeable that hadn't existed in the
Moscow insurrection: the wall between the two camps – the people
and the authorities – was not so impenetrable; a certain diffusion
could be felt between them. This increased the excitement and
40 filled the masses with something like enthusiasm.
       N. N. Sukhanov, *The Russian Revolution 1917. A Personal
       Record* (1955) p 16

(c) Mutinies

It became clear later that what had happened was this: A small
detachment of mounted police had orders to disperse a crowd that
had collected along the Catherine Canal; for safety's sake the police
began to fire on it from the opposite bank, across the canal. Just
45 then a detachment of Pavlovskys was passing along the bank that
was occupied by the crowd. It was then than an historic incident
took place that marked an abrupt break in the course of events and
opened up new perspectives for the movement: seeing this shooting
at unarmed people and the wounded falling around them and
50 finding themselves in the zone of fire, the Pavlovskys opened fire
at the police across the canal.
   This was the first instance of a massive open clash between armed
detachments. It was described to us in detail by a friend who came
to Gorky's later on; he had been walking along the Catherine Canal
55 at the time and had personally seen the wounded policemen and
their bloodstained horses. Then the Pavlovskys, now 'mutineers'
who had burnt their boats, returned to their barracks and appealed
to their comrades to join them. This was when the firing took
place between the loyal and the rebel parts of the regiment. How
60 far all this was deliberate on the part of the Pavlovskys and how
far it was the result of momentary instinct, nervous impulse, and
simple self-defence, it is impossible to say. But the objective
importance of this affair at the Catherine Canal was enormous and
quite unmistakable. In any case, to the Pavlovsky Regiment belongs
65 the honour of having performed the first revolutionary act of the
military against the armed forces of Tsarism.
   It was obvious that there could be no talk of a conclusive victory
for the revolution without a victory over the army and the
transference of the greater part of it to the side of the revolutionary
70 populace. And the Pavlovsky Regiment had made a beginning on
the evening of February 26th.
       Ibid, pp 28–9

(d) Revolution

Ivanov's questions:

1. How many troops are in order and how many are misbehaving?

Khabalov's replies:

1. I have at my disposal in the Admiralty building four companies of the Guard, five squadrons of cavalry and Cossacks, and two batteries; the rest of the troops have gone over to the revolutionists, or by agreement with them are remaining neutral. Soldiers are wandering through the town singly or in bands disarming officers.

2. Which railroad stations are guarded?

2. All the stations are in the hands of the revolutionists and strictly guarded by them.

3. In what parts of the city is order preserved?

3. The whole city is in the hands of the revolutionists. The telephone is not working, there is no communication between different parts of the city.

4. What authorities are governing the different parts of the city?

4. I cannot answer this question.

5. Are all the ministries functioning properly?

5. The ministers have been arrested by the revolutionists.

6. What police forces are at your disposal at the present moment?

6. None whatever.

7. What technical and supply institutions of the War Department are now in your control?

7. I have none.

8. What quantity of provisions is at your disposal?

8. There are no provisions at my disposal. In the city on February 5, there were 5,600,000 pounds of flour in the store.

9. Have many weapons, artillery and military stores fallen into the hands of the mutineers?

9. All the artillery establishments are in the hands of the revolutionists.

10. What military forces and staffs are in your control?	10. The chief of the Staff of the District is in my personal control. With the other district administrations I have no connections.

120

Trotsky, *My Life*, op cit, pp 84–5

Questions

a According to extract (a), what happened in Petrograd on February 23?

b In extract (b), why did there appear more possibility of a revolution in February 1917 than in 1905?

c Why does the author of extract (c) claim that the Pavlovsky Regiment committed 'the first revolutionary act of the military against the armed forces of Tsarism' (lines 66–7)?

d Do the events described in this extract appear planned or accidental?

e What does extract (d) show? Why was it written in this way?

(e) Rioting

'At last! At last!' shouted a demonstrator, pointing at a red glow in the direction of the Nicolaevsky station.

'What is burning?'

'The police station.'

5   'But there is a fire station in the same building.'

'That won't help. We are going to destroy all government offices, burn, smash, kill all police, all tyrants, all despots.'

On the Liteiny a new blaze breaks out and is unchecked. It is the Okroujny Soud, the magnificent building of the High Court
10 of Justice.

'Who started that fire?' someone asks. 'Is it not necessary to have a court building for new Russia?'

As the frenzy spreads, rioters and looters fall on their natural enemies, the policemen. The Social Revolutionary, Pitrim Sorokin,
15 tells us that he came on a group of men pitilessly beating a prostrate policeman with butts of revolvers and grinding their victim's body into the pavement with their boot heels. 'Stop that, you brutes!' cried Sorokin's companion. 'Arrest the man if you like, but don't kill him.'
20 'Who are you to hinder us from killing a Pharaoh?' the mob yelled. 'Are you also a counter-revolutionary?'

A few moments later, from a window on the fourth floor of a house where a Tzarist general lodged, a man was tossed to the pavement beneath by revolting soldiers. His piercing shriek of

25 agony was drowned by shouts of exultation. 'As the body crashed
    on the stones,' Sorokin writes, 'men rushed forward, stamping on
    it, lashing it with whatever they held in their hands. Deathly sick
    with the hideousness of the sight, I ran on, my companion
    following.' . . . But someone plucked desperately at his sleeve:
30 'Sorokin! I know you are generous. Save me! In the name of God,
    save me.' In this trembling fugitive Sorokin recognized a spy of
    the Secret Service who, two years previously, had denounced and
    secured the arrest of the very man from whom he was now begging
    sanctuary. 'Go home quickly,' answered Sorokin. 'Destroy your
35 uniform and then, if you can, change your lodging. . . . If anything
    happens, let me know.'

    Edmund A. Walsh, *The Fall of the Russian Empire* (1929)
    p 101

(f) An outsider's view

As we came out of the ministry, Sir George Buchanan said to me:
    'Let's go by the Court Quay instead of going through the
    Millionaia. We shall avoid the Guard's barracks that way.'
40 But as we entered the quay we were recognized by a body of
    students who cheered us and provided an escort. Opposite the
    Marble Palace the crowd got much larger and noisily enthusiastic.
    Cries of 'Long live the Internationale! Long live peace!' blended
    unpleasantly with shouts of 'Long live France! Long live England!'
45 At the corner of Suvorov Square, Buchanan left me after advising
    me to take shelter in his embassy from the mob, which was getting
    somewhat too excited. But as it was late and I wanted to wire to
    Paris before lunch, I went on my way. Opposite the Summer
    Garden I was entirely surrounded by the crowd which stopped a
50 passing motor machine-gun and insisted on my getting in and
    being conveyed to the Tauride Palace. A huge and boisterous
    student, waving a red flag, bawled in my face in excellent French:
    'Pay your respects to the Russian Revolution! The red flag is
    Russia's flag now; do homage to it in the name of France!'
55 He translated his words into Russian and they were greeted with
    frantic cheers. I replied:
    'I cannot pay a finer tribute to Russian liberty than to invite you
    to join me in saying: "Long live the war!"'
    He was very careful not to translate my reply. At length we
60 reached the embassy. Not without considerable trouble and the
    strenuous efforts of my chasseur did I succeed in getting clear of
    the crowd and within my own doors.

    Maurice Paléologue, *An Ambassador's Memoirs 1914–17*
    (1973) p 819

(g) Revolutionary demands

Near the entrance to the Letopis offices, at the gates of the neighbouring factory, I met a small group of civilians, workers by
65 the look of them.

'What do they want?' said one grim-looking fellow. 'They want bread, peace with the Germans, and equality for the Yids.'

Sukhanov, op cit, p 17

Questions

a What types of people are being attacked in extract (e) and why?
b What impression of the revolution is given by extract (e)?
c How does the view of the revolution in extract (f) differ from that in extract (e)?
d Why do you think the author of extract (f) wrote the line: 'He was very careful not to translate my reply' (line 59)?
★ e How good a summary of the revolutionaries' demands are those mentioned in extract (g)?

3 The Downfall of the Tsar

(a) The tsar's character

The tzar's outlook was not broader than that of a minor police official – with this difference, that the latter would have a better knowledge of reality and be less burdened with superstitions. The sole paper which Nicholas read for years, and from which he
5 derived his ideas, was a weekly published on state revenue by Prince Meschersky, a vile, bribed journalist of the reactionary bureaucratic clique, despised even in his own circle. The tzar kept his outlook unchanged through two wars and two revolutions. Between his consciousness and events stood always that
10 impenetrable medium – indifference. Nicholas was called, not without foundation, a fatalist. It is only necessary to add that his fatalism was the exact opposite of an active belief in his 'star'. Nicholas indeed considered himself unlucky. His fatalism was only a form of passive self-defense against historic evolution, and
15 went hand in hand with an arbitrariness, trivial in psychological motivation, but monstrous in its consequences.

'I wish it and therefore it must be—' writes Count Witte. 'That motto appeared in all the activities of this weak rule, who only through weakness did all the things which characterized his reign –
20 a wholesale shedding of more or less innocent blood, for the most part without aim.'

Trotsky, *The Russian Revolution*, op cit, pp 54–5

(b) Telegram from the Duma to Nicholas II

The sessions of the State Duma, by order of Your Majesty, have been broken off until April. The last bulwark of order has been removed. The Government is completely powerless to suppress
25 disorder. The troops of the garrison are unreliable. The reserve battalions of the Guard regiments are caught up by the revolt. They kill their officers. Joining the mob and the popular movement they advance to the building of the Ministry of Internal Affairs and to the State Duma. Civil war has begun and blazes up. Give orders
30 immediately to summon a new government on the basis outlined to Your Majesty in my telegram of yesterday. Give orders to abrogate your Imperial decree and to convoke again the legislative chambers. Proclaim these measures immediately by Imperial Manifesto. Do not delay, Sire. If the movement spreads to the army the
35 German will triumph, and the fall of Russia, and with it of the dynasty, is inevitable. In the name of all Russia I implore Your Majesty to fulfill these suggestions. The hour which will decide your fate and that of the motherland has struck. Tomorrow may be already too late.

> Quoted in William Henry Chamberlain, *The Russian Revolution*, vol I (New York, 1965) p 429

(c) The Act of Abdication of the Czar Nicholas II

40 By the Grace of God, We, Nicholas II. Emperor of all the Russias, Tsar of Poland, Grand-Duke of Finland, etc., etc. . . . to all Our faithful subjects make known:

In these days of terrible struggle against the external enemy who has been trying for three years to impose his will upon Our
45 Fatherland, God has willed that Russia should be faced with a new and formidable trial. Troubles at home threaten to have a fatal effect on the ultimate course of this hard-fought war. The destinies of Russia, the honour of Our heroic army, the welfare of the people and the whole future of Our dear country demand that the war
50 should be carried to a victorious conclusion at any price.

Our cruel foe is making his supreme effort, and the moment is at hand in which Our valiant army, in concert with Our glorious allies, will overthrow him once and for all.

In these days, which are decisive for the existence of Russia, We
55 think We should follow the voice of Our conscience by facilitating the closest co-operation of Our people and the organisation of all its resources for the speedy realisation of victory.

For these reasons, in accord with the Duma of the Empire, We think it Our duty to abdicate the Crown and lay down the supreme
60 power.

Not desiring to be separated from Our beloved son, We bequeath Our heritage to Our brother, the Grand Duke Michael Alexandrovitch, and give him Our blessing. We abjure him to govern in perfect accord with the representatives of the nation sitting in the
65 legislative institutions, and to take a sacred oath in the name of the beloved Fatherland.

We appeal to all the loyal sons of the country, imploring them to fulfil their patriotic and holy duty of obeying their Czar in this sad time of national trial. We ask them to help him and the
70 representatives of the nation to guide the Russian state into the path of prosperity and glory.

God help Russia.

Gilliard, op cit, pp 196–7

(d) Another opinion of the tsar

Scrutinising this living mask, I began to understand why the reins of government had slipped so easily out of his hands. He bore 'the
75 burden of power' until the end. But he would not fight for it: he had no wish to rule. Power, like everything else that was earthly and consequently humdrum, bored him, tired him, and no longer thrilled. He calmly laid aside his sceptre to take up a gardener's spade. Just as Dubensky said: he gave up the throne like handing
80 over a troop of horse: threw aside the Imperial purple as in his youth he tossed aside one splendid military uniform to put on another. And now he found it an interesting experience to be without a uniform at all – just an ordinary citizen, free of all duties and obligations. Without any inner drama – 'It was God's will,' he
85 said – he stepped out into private life. Indeed, all those who observed him closely during his 'captivity' assert unanimously, that throughout this period the former Emperor was generally in a calm and even happy mood.

Alexander Kerensky, *The Road to the Tragedy* (Hutchinson, 1935) p 125

Questions

a   What is Trotsky's opinion of the tsar, according to extract (a)?
b   What advice is given to the tsar in extract (b)? Why did this advice need to be given?
c   According to extract (c), why had the tsar decided to abdicate?
d   What is Kerensky's assessment of Nicholas II in extract (d)? How does this compare with the conclusion of extract (a)?
★ e   Why did Russia cease to be ruled by the tsars?

4 Why did the February Revolution occur?

(a) A Social Revolutionary view

Neither the Bolsheviks, nor the Mensheviks, nor the Workers' Group, nor the Social Revolutionaries, either separately or collectively, led the workers of Petrograd on to the street. It was someone mightier than they: Tsar Hunger.

5   It began with ordinary food riots. The bakeshops lacked sufficient bread. Long queues, at first chiefly of women and boys, took out their resentment on the bakers, suspecting them of hoarding flour for purposes of speculation. The police restored order. They were greeted with hostile shouts. The people demanded 'Bread!' Then

10   naturally they began to shout, 'Down with the police!' But as soon as the thousand-voiced echo caught this up, there appeared the old slogans, 'Down with the autocracy!' and 'Down with the war!' There were disorders, there was still no revolution. There was no leader, but every revolutionary and democratic group, organized

15   or unorganized, rushed headlong into the movement, trying to attract as many people as possible and to inspire it with definite and militant political slogans.

        Chernov, op cit, p 101

(b) A communist view

Before the revolution the liberal leader had declared every thought of revolution a suggestion of the German Staff. But the situation

20   was more complicated after a revolution which had brought the liberals to power. Miliukov's task was now not to dishonor the revolution with a Hohenzollern origin, but on the contrary to withhold the honor of its initiation from revolutionists. Liberalism therefore has whole-heartedly fathered the theory of a spontaneous

25   and impersonal revolution. Miliukov sympathetically cites the semi-liberal, semi-socialist Stankevich, a university instructor who became Political Commissar at the headquarters of the Supreme Command: 'The masses moved of themselves, obeying some unaccountable inner summons . . .' writes Stankevich of the Febru-

30   ary days. 'With what slogans did the soldiers come out? Who led them when they conquered Petrograd, when they burned the District Court? Not a political idea, not a revolutionary slogan, not a conspiracy, and not a revolt, but a spontaneous movement suddenly consuming the entire old power to the last remnant.'

35   Spontaneousness here acquires an almost mystic character.

        Trotsky, *The Russian Revolution*, op cit, pp 142–3

(c) British views (i)

During the attempts at revolution in 1906 I wrote: 'Speaking of
the Russian Empire which Nicholas II received from his father,
Alexander III, one may say with as much certitude as such
contingent judgements admit, that it could have been governed at
40   least for another forty or fifty years without a constitution. But on
condition that it was governed. The Prussians of the days of
Frederick the Great were much more intelligent than the Russians
of today, yet they enjoyed absolutism and throve under it. But
then although absolute it was really government, and justice was
45   its basis. The Russians of today – the masses of benighted peasantry –
are unfitted to govern the Empire, and for that reason a strong
autocracy might have long continued in power. But even peasants
will not endure starvation by inches, which was what absolutism
offered to many of them. Like the worm, the mooshik will turn
50   when trodden on. The Russian people now demand a constitution,
not because the bureaucracy is no longer capable of carrying on
the system of absolutism. . . . To the will of the nation the
government can oppose only the bayonets of the troops, and even
the tempered steel of bayonet will not long support a throne devoid
55   of all other props. And that is now the relative position of the
autocracy and the army.

> E. J. Dillon, *The Eclipse of Russia* (1918) pp 386–7

(d) British views (ii)

No one made the Russian Revolution, unless it was the autocracy
itself; certainly no one on the other side, if one excepts the last-
minute change round of the Volynsky regiment. Till then there
60   was no organised opposition to the police and troops, and,
indeed, that very evening, at a meeting of revolutionary leaders in
Kerensky's quarters, it was precisely the Bolsheviks present who
said that the moment had not yet come and that succeess was not
to be hoped for. The moment came in the Volynsky barracks a
65   few hours later. Lenin and all the principal Bolshevik leaders were
not in Russia; Lenin and his nearest colleagues were in Switzerland.
Their influence on Russia at this time was only now beginning to
be of serious significance, and their pledged supporters probably
did not number more than fifteen thousand. Neither did the Duma
70   do anything to make the Revolution; when it came, nearly everyone
there except Kerensky was scared by it. It was elemental, and for
that reason all the more conclusive. It was a direct result of the
utter bankruptcy of the autocracy, and for that reason it was
irrevocable.

> Bernard Pares, *Russia* (1940) p 100

(e) British views (iii)

75 An immense and extremely valuable work was done by the so-
called public organizations, represented by the Union of Cities and
by the Union of Zemstvos, in providing the army with a whole
network of hospitals and factories. Without this aid, the Russian
military machine would have broken down far sooner than it did.
80 Yet, instead of stimulating this patriotic effort and encouraging the
public organizations in every way it could, the Russian Government
did its best to hamper and curtail its activities. It may be said that
the public organizations were politically ambitious, that they were
honeycombed with Liberalism and therefore a menace to the
85 autocracy. . . .
But in the beginning at any rate, their enthusiasm for the war
was single-minded, and the political aspirations, which came later,
were the direct result of a policy of perpetual pin-pricks. It was the
tragedy of Russia that the Tsar, dominated by a woman who was
90 obsessed with the one ambition to hand down the autocracy
unimpaired to her son, never took the public organisations into his
confidence. The fact that gradually Moscow became more absorbed
in the internal political struggle than in the war itself was mainly
the result of the Tsar's fatal obtuseness. And, although his loyalty
95 to his Allies remained unshaken to the last, it was his failure to
harness the loyalty of his own people which eventually cost him
his throne.

Lockhart, op cit, pp 100–1

Questions

a According to extract (a), how did food riots lead to revolution?
b In extract (b), explain the sentence 'Liberalism . . . has whole-
heartedly fathered the theory of a spontaneous and impersonal
revolution' (lines 23–5).
★ *c* Why might a communist like Trotsky support the idea that the
revolution was spontaneous and unplanned?
d Why was there a revolution according to extract (c)?
e Explain the comment in extract (d): 'No one made the Russian
Revolution, unless it was the autocracy itself' (line 58).
f Why does the author of extract (e) blame the tsar for the
February Revolution?
★ *g* Why did the February Revolution take place?

III   *The Provisional Government (i) February–June*

Introduction

The sudden departure of the tsar left a vacuum in Russian politics, one which a number of competing interests tried to fill. The most obvious candidate was the Duma, Russia's parliament. Nicholas II had tried to dissolve it at the start of the unrest but a good proportion of its members had disobeyed this command. Conscious of their narrow base support – very few people had the vote at this time – they called themselves a Provisional Government and immediately announced plans for the calling of a Constituent Assembly based on universal suffrage: but this would take some months to organise.

At the same time the reforming of elected councils of workers, peasants and soldiers, the soviets, created another form of government emphasised by the fact that their famous Order Number One informed their supporters that the Soviet took precedence over the Provisional Government. In fact the threat was more apparent than real. Almost all political parties supported the government at first, fearing as they did the possibility of counter-revolution. Even the Bolsheviks, admittedly hampered by the absence of many of their leaders in exile, gave initial support. According to Marxist theory, the Bourgeois revolution had taken place in February; it would be some time before the Proletarian revolution could occur.

All this changed with the return of Lenin to Russia. He argued that the proletarian revolution was already occurring as the soldiers deserted from the armies, the peasants seized the land. It was wrong for the Bolsheviks to prop up the government. Instead, they should spread propaganda amongst the workers and peasants in preparation for the forthcoming seizure of power.

Lenin admitted that this would take a little time. As yet the Bolsheviks were still a minority, even in the Soviets, and no threat to the Provisional Government, especially when the latter had the tacit support of most other parties. Unfortunately the government had few ideas of its own. It felt that it could not hand the land to the peasants or organise proper food supplies until the war had ended; and with Russia doing so badly, it was hardly the best time to end the war. Lvov, Kerensky and the others therefore decided to continue fighting in the vain hope that a change of government would compensate for a total lack of improvements in either military equipment or leadership.

1 Rival Governments

(a) An overview: 14 March 1917

In the general anarchy which is raging in Petrograd two directing bodies are in process of formation:

(1) The 'Executive Committee of the Duma,' with Rodzianko as its president and comprising twelve members, including Miliukov,
5 Shulgin, Konovalov, Kerensky and Cheidze. It is thus representative of all parties of the progressive group and the Extreme Left. It is trying to secure the necessary reforms immediately in order to maintain the existing political system, at the cost of proclaiming another emperor, if need be. But the Tauris Palace is occupied by
10 the insurgents so that the committee has to confer amidst general uproar, and is exposed to the bullying of the mob; (2) The 'Council of Working-Men and Soldier Deputies,' the Soviet. It holds its sittings at the Finland station. Its password and battlecry is 'Proclaim the social Republic and put an end to the war.' Its leaders are
15 already denouncing the members of the Duma as traitors to the revolution.

Paléologue, op cit, pp 822–3

(b) Forming the Provisional Government

Without any previous arrangement the members of the Duma straggled from the session hall into the adjoining semi-circular hall. This was not a meeting of the Duma which had just ended, nor
20 was it a session of one of its committees. It was a private conference of the Duma members. The solitary individuals who had loitered in the other halls, began to approach the group which had gathered. I do not remember whether Rodzianko acted as chairman; the meeting was amorphous; heated speeches sounded forth from the
25 group in the middle. Proposals were made to return and re-open a formal session of the Duma, refusing to recognize the decree (M. A. Karavalov); to declare the Duma a Constituent Assembly and to turn over authority to a dictator (General Manikovosky); to take power with those gathered there and create our own body – in any
30 event, not to disperse and leave Petersburg. I proposed to wait awhile until the character of the disturbances became clearer, and, in the meantime, to create a temporary committee of Duma members 'for restoring order and maintaining contact with various persons and institutions.' This awkward formula had the advantage

35 of meeting the problem of the moment without determining anything for the future. Limiting itself to the minimum, it created a working body but did not lead the Duma Members into criminal action. Stormy protests rang forth from the left, but the meeting as a whole did not waver. After long arguments my compromise
40 proposal was adopted, and the election of a 'Temporary Committee' was entrusted to the Council of Elders. This meant transferring it to the bloc. At three o'clock in the afternoon, the Elders carried out their task, nominating representatives of the bloc parties to the committee. It should be added that this choice partially determined
45 the composition of the future government. First of all, the members of the Duma presidium entered the committee (Rodzianko, Dmitriukov, Rzhevsky); then there came the representatives of the factions; Shulgin (from the nationalists) V. I. Lvov (from the center), Shidlovsky (from the Octobrists), Miliukov and Nekrasov, the
50 deputy chairman (from the Kadets); the leftists Kerensky and Chkheidze also adhered to the project.

Paul Miliukov, *Political Memoirs 1905–17* (Michigan, 1967) p 391

(c) Forming Soviets

The Mensheviks liberated from prison, members of the Military–Industrial Committee, meeting in the Tauride Palace with leaders of the Trade Union and cooperative movements, likewise of the
55 right wing, and with the Menshevik deputies of the Duma, Cheidze and Skobelev, straightway formed a 'Provisional Executive Committee of the Soviet of Workers' Deputies,' which in the course of the day was filled out principally with former revolutionists who had lost connection with the masses but still preserved their 'names.'
60 This Executive Committee, including also Bolsheviks in its staff, summoned the workers to elect deputies at once. The first session was appointed for the same evening in the Tauride Palace. . . . But in here lay the significance of this first meeting of representatives of the victorious proletariat of the capital. Delegates from the
65 mutinied regiments made speeches of greeting at this meeting. Among their number were completely gray soldiers, shell-shocked as it were by the insurrection, and still hardly in control of their tongues. But they were just the ones who found the words which no orator could find. . . .
70 At this first session it was decided to unite the garrison with the workers in a general Soviet of Workers' and Soldiers.
. . . From the moment of its formation the Soviet, in the person of its Executive Committee, begins to function as a sovereign. It elects a temporary food commission and places it in charge of the
75 mutineers and of the garrison in general. . . .
The tasks and functions of the Soviet grow unceasingly under

pressure from the masses. The revolution finds here its indubitable center. The workers, the soldiers, and soon also the peasants, will from now on turn only to the Soviet. In their eyes the Soviet becomes the focus of all hopes and all authority, an incarnation of the revolution itself.

However, even in those very first days of victory, when the new power of the revolution was forming itself with fabulous speed and inconquerable strength, those socialists who stood at the head of the Soviet were already looking around with alarm to see if they could find a real 'boss.' They took it for granted that the power ought to pass to the bourgeoisie. Here the chief political knot of the new regime is tied: one of its threads leads into the chamber of the Executive Committee of workers and soldiers, the other into the central headquarters of the bourgeois parties.

Trotsky, *The Russian Revolution*, op cit, pp 158–9

(d) Order Number One

March 1st 1917

To the garrison of the Petrograd District. To all the soldiers of the Guard, army, artillery and fleet for immediate and precise execution, and to the workers of Petrograd for information.

The Soviet Workers' and Soldiers' Deputies has decided:

1. In all companies, battalions, regiments, depots, batteries, squadrons and separate branches of military service of every kind and on warships immediately choose committees from the elected representatives of the soldiers and sailors of the above mentioned military units.

2. In all military units which have still not elected their representatives in the Soviet of Workers' Deputies elect one representative to a Company, who should appear with written credentials in the building of the State Duma at ten o'clock on the morning of March 2.

3. In all its political demonstrations a military unit is subordinated to the Soviet of Workers' and Soldiers' Deputies and its committees.

4. The orders of the military commission of the State Duma are to be fulfilled only in those cases which do not contradict the orders and decisions of the Soviet of Workers' and Soldiers' Deputies.

5. Arms of all kinds, as rifles, machine-guns, armoured automobiles and others must be at the dispositions and under the control of the company and battalion committees and are not in any case to be given out to officers, even upon their demand.

6. In the ranks and in fulfilling service duties soldiers must observe the strictest military discipline; but outside of service, in their political, civil and private life soldiers cannot be discriminated against as regards those rights which all citizens enjoy.

Standing at attention and compulsory saluting outside of service
120 are especially abolished.

7. In the same way the addressing of officers with titles: Your
Excellency, Your Honor, etc., is abolished and is replaced by the
forms of address: Mr. General, Mr. Colonel, etc.

Rude treatment of soldiers of all ranks, and especially addressing
125 them as 'thou', is forbidden; and soldiers are bound to bring to the
attention of the company committees any violation of this rule and
any misunderstandings between officers and soldiers.

This order is to be read in all companies, battalions, regiments,
marine units, batteries and other front and rear military units.
130 PETROGRAD SOVIET OF WORKERS' AND SOLDIERS'
DEPUTIES.
Quoted in Chamberlain, vol I, op cit, pp 429–30

(e) Criticism

Order No. 1 was a charter to the troops absolving them from the
necessity of obeying any orders which they had not previously
discussed among themselves and approved, and was completely
135 incompatible with the waging of a war. The Russian army was
paralysed, robbed at one stroke of the power of brain over limb,
of the co-operation of limb with limb, of the ability to move an
inch in concert without a referendum of seven million men.
Through their class–conscious hesitations over joining in a revol-
140 ution initiated from below, the Russian officer class had thrown
away their right to leadership of the army in revolt and made the
inspiration of the rank and file committee system of Order No. 1
inevitable. Class distrust, class hatred, class warfare had been born,
but it had been engendered, so far as the army was concerned,
145 from above.

If the right of free speech was a lovely new toy to the people in
general, the committee rule set up by Order No. 1 was at first an
equally lovely plaything of their own to the soldiers in the garrisons
and at the front. They deposed and elected officers with the
150 enthusiasm and fickleness of girls choosing leaders for their games
at school. One of the Petrograd battalions chose three commanding
officers in one day.
Dorian Blair and C. H. Dand, *Russian Hazzard* (1939) p 113

Questions

a According to extract (a), what are the differences between the
two directing bodies?

b With reference to extract (b), why do you think the Provisional
Government was so called?

c Which political parties are mentioned in this extract, and which
are not?

d In extract (c) who is responsible for setting up the Soviets in Petrograd?

e In what ways does Trotsky criticise the leaders of the Soviets?

f How does Order Number One, in extract (d), challenge the authority of the Provisional Government?

g How does this order seek to affect the armed forces of Russia?

h In what ways does extract (e) seek both to criticise and to patronise the makers of Order Number One?

★ *i* Why is this order seen as being important by some observers at this time?

2 Bolshevik Reactions

(a) Party problems

How was it with the Bolsheviks? This we have in part already seen. The principal leaders of the underground Bolshevik organization were at that time three men; the former workers Shliapnikov and Zalutsky, and the former student Molotov. Shliapnikov,
5 having lived for some time abroad and in close association with Lenin, was in a political sense the most mature and active of these three who constituted the Bureau of the Central Committee. However, Shliapnikov's own memoirs best of all confirm the fact that the events were too much for the trio. . . .
10   The weakness of the underground organizations was a direct result of police raids, which had given exceptional results amid the patriotic moods at the beginning of the war.

In order to get a clear conception of the situation in the sphere of revolutionary leadership it is necessary to remember that the
15 most authoritative revolutionists, the leaders of the left parties, were abroad and, some of them, in prison and exile. The more dangerous a party was to the old regime, the most cruelly beheaded it appeared at the moment of revolution. The Narodniks had a Duma faction headed by the non-party radical Kerensky. The
20 official leader of the Social-Revolutionaries, Chernov, was abroad. The Mensheviks had a party faction in the Duma headed by Cheidze and Skobelev; Martov was abroad; Dun and Tseretelli, in exile. The Bolsheviks had no faction; their five worker-deputies, in whom the tzarist government had seen the organizing center of the
25 revolution, had been arrested during the first few months of the war. Lenin was abroad, Zinoviev with him; Kamenev was in exile; in exile also, the then little known practical leaders; Sverdlov, Rykov, Stalin. The Polish social-democrat, Dzerzhinsky, who did not yet belong to the Bolsheviks, was at hard labor. The leaders
30 accidentally present, for the very reason that they had been accustomed to act under unconditionally authoritative supervisors, did not consider themselves and were not considered by others

capable of playing a guiding role in revolutionary events.
Trotsky, *The Russian Revolution*, op cit, pp 144–5

(b) The Bolsheviks: first responses

Even so firm a Bolshevik as Stalin said at the party conference on
35 March 27:
'The Provisional Government has in fact undertaken to intrench
the conquests of the revolutionary people. The Soviet of Workers'
and Soldiers' Deputies mobilizes forces, supervises; the Provisional
Government, albeit restively, confusedly, intrenches the conquests
40 which the people have already won in fact. Such a situation has
both negative and positive sides: at present it is not advantageous
for us to force events and thus hasten the secession of the bourgeois
strata which later must inevitably break with us.'
In this form Bolshevism could be only a radically tinged
45 appendage to the Social Democratic front as a whole, and till
Lenin's arrival it was just that. At the Petrograd Menshevist city
conference, early in March, the question of fusion with the
Bolsheviks was on the agenda. At the Bolshevist conference in
March Stalin urged that they respond to Tseretelli's fusion pro-
50 posals, since 'to look too far ahead and anticipate disagreements
was wrong'; they could be 'overcome within the party.' In the
question of the war at first 'the Bolsheviks, properly speaking,
advanced no independent program.' Stalin said in so many
words, 'The mere slogan – "Down with war!" – is absolutely
55 useless as a practical tool.' In mid-March Kamenev returned from
Siberia. He and Stalin took over the leadership of the Bolshevist
faction in the Soviet and the editing of its central newspaper,
Pravda. However, this did not create a gulf between Bolshevism
and the central leadership of the Soviet, but rather the contrary.
60 *Pravda* dropped its recklessly demagogic tone. Even in the burning
question of the war it asserted that 'the war will go on, for the
German army has not yet followed the example of the Russian
army and still obeys its emperor; under such circumstances, for the
Russian soldiers 'to disperse to their homes would be a policy, not
65 of peace but of slavery, a policy which the free Russian people will
reject with indignation.' The newspaper defended the necessity 'for
replying to each bullet by a bullet and to each shell by a shell,'
without permitting 'any disorganization of the revolution's military
forces.' While demanding the opening of negotiations 'to find a
70 way to end the World War,' Pravda constantly insisted that 'till
then each must stick to his post.'
All this was not far from the official position of the Menshevist
and Social Revolutionary majority. Indeed, at about that time (late
March or early April) 'a joint meeting of Mensheviks and Bolsheviks
75 was arranged, at which the question of unification was touched

upon incidentally.' Previously, in Moscow 'at the party (Bolshevist) conference, among other matters, the question was brought up of the possibility of uniting with the Mensheviks, since in the provinces there was a rather strong urge to that.' The fusion negotiations dragged along till Lenin's return from abroad quickly put a stop to them. At that time Lenin remarked ironically that he knew of only two real Bolsheviks: himself and his wife.

Chernov, op cit, pp 412–13

Questions

a   With reference to extract (a), why did the Bolsheviks not react decisively at first to the February revolution?

★ b   Why were the leaders of many of Russia's political parties in exile at this time?

c   According to extract (b), what was the initial Bolshevik response to: the Provisional Government; the war; other parties?

★ d   Stalin was a relatively unimportant person at this time. Why do you think he is given such prominence in this extract?

(c) *Lenin returns to Russia*

Lenin came, or rather ran, into the room. He wore a round cap, his face looked frozen, and there was a magnificent bouquet in his hands. Running to the middle of the room, he stopped in front of Chkheidze as though colliding with a completely unexpected obstacle. And Chkheidze, still glum, pronounced the following 'speech of welcome' with not only the spirit and wording but also the tone of a sermon:

'Comrade Lenin, in the name of the Petersburg Soviet and of the whole revolution we welcome you to Russia. . . . But – we think that the principal task of the revolutionary democracy is now the defence of the revolution from any encroachments either from within or from without. We consider that what this goal requires is not disunion, but the closing of the democratic ranks. We hope you will pursue these goals together with us.'

Chkheidze stopped speaking. I was dumbfounded with surprise: really, what attitude could be taken to this 'welcome' and to that delicious 'But – '?

But Lenin plainly knew exactly how to behave. He stood there as though nothing taking place had the slightest connection with him – looking about him, examining the persons around him and even the ceiling of the imperial waiting-room, adjusting his bouquet (rather out of tune with his whole appearance), and then, turning away from the Ex. Com. delegation altogether, he made his 'reply':

'Dear Comrades, soldiers, sailors, and workers! I am happy to greet in your persons the victorious Russian revolution, and greet

you as the vanguard of the worldwide proletarian army. . . . The piratical imperialist war is the beginning of civil war throughout Europe. . . . The hour is not far distant when at the call of our comrade, Karl Liebknecht, the peoples will turn their arms against
30　their own capitalist exploiters. . . . The worldwide Socialist revolution has already dawned. . . . Germany is seething. . . . Any day now the whole of European capitalism may crash. The Russian revolution accomplished by you has prepared the way and opened a new epoch. Long live the worldwide Socialist revolution!'
35　　This was really no reply to Chkheidze's 'welcome', and it entirely failed to echo the 'context' of the Russian revolution as accepted by everyone, without distinction, of its witnesses and participants.
　　　　　Sukhanov, op cit, pp 272–3

(d) The April Theses

1. The specific feature of the present situation in Russia is that the country is passing from the first stage of the revolution – which,
40　owing to the insufficient class-consciousness and organisation of the proletariat, placed power in the hands of the bourgeoisie – to its second stage, which must place power in the hands of the proletariat and the poorest sections of the peasants.

　　This transition is characterised, on the one hand, by a maximum
45　of legally recognised rights (Russia is now the freest of all the belligerent countries in the world); on the other, by the absence of violence towards the masses, and, finally, by their unreasoning trust in the government of capitalists, those worst enemies of peace and socialism.
50　　This peculiar situation demands of us an ability to adapt ourselves to the special conditions of Party work among unprecedently large masses of proletarians who have just awakened to political life.
2. No support for the Provisional Government, the utter falsity of all its promises should be made clear, particularly of those relating
55　to the renunciation of annexations. Exposure in place of the impermissible, illusion-breeding 'demand' that this government, a government of capitalists, should cease to be an imperialist government.
3. Recognition of the fact that in most of the Soviets of Workers'
60　Deputies our Party is in a minority, so far a small minority, as against a bloc of all the petty-bourgeois opportunist elements, from the Popular Socialists and the Socialist-Revolutionaries down to the Organising Committee (Chkheidze, Tsereteli, etc.), Steklov, etc., etc., who have yielded to the influence of the bourgeoisie and
65　spread that influence among the proletariat.

　　The masses must be made to see that the Soviets of Workers' Deputies are the only possible form of revolutionary government, and that therefore our task is, as long as this government yields to

the influence of the bourgeoisie, to present a patient, systematic, and
70　persistent explanation of the errors of their tactics, an explanation
especially adapted to the practical needs of the masses.

4. Not a parliamentary republic – to return to a parliamentary
republic from the Soviets of Workers' Deputies would be a
retrograde step – but a republic of Soviets of Workers', Agricultural
75　Labourers' and Peasants' Deputies throughout the country, from
top to bottom.

Abolition of the police, the army and the bureaucracy. The
salaries of all officials, all of whom are elective and displaceable at
any time, not to exceed the average wage of a competent worker.
80　5. The weight of emphasis is the agrarian programme to be shifted
to the Soviets of Agricultural Labourers' Deputies.

Confiscation of all landed estates.

Nationalisation of all lands in the country, the land to be disposed
of by the local Soviets of Agricultural Labourers' and Peasants'
85　Deputies. . . .

6. The immediate amalgamation of all banks in the country into a
single national bank, and the institution of control over it by the
Soviet of Workers' Deputies.

Lenin, *The April Theses* (Moscow, 1976) pp 8–9

(e) Lenin's theories

Beginning with February 1917, however, long before the October
90　Revolution, that is, long before we assumed power, we publicly
declared and explained to the people: the revolution cannot now
stop at this stage, for the country has marched forward, capitalism
has advanced, ruin has reached fantastic dimensions, which
(whether one likes it or not) will demand steps forward, to
95　socialism. For there is no other way of advancing, of saving the
war-weary country and of alleviating the sufferings of the working
and exploited people.

Things have turned out just as we said they would. The course
taken by the revolution has confirmed the correctness of our
100　reasoning. First, with the 'whole' of the peasants against the
monarchy, against the landowners, against medievalism (and to that
extent the revolution remains bourgeois, bourgeois–democratic).
Then, with the poor peasants, with the semi-proletarians, with all
the exploited, against capitalism, including the rural rich, the
105　kulaks, the profiteers, and to that extent, the revolution becomes a
socialist one. To attempt to raise an artificial Chinese Wall between
the first and second, to separate them by anything else than the
degree of preparedness of the proletariat and the degree of its unity
with the poor peasants, means to distort Marxism dreadfully, to
110　vulgarise it, to substitute liberalism in its place.

Lenin, *The Proletarian Revolution and the Renegade Kautsky.*

Quoted in Lenin, *On the Great October Socialist Revolution* (Moscow, 1976)

(f) Revised Bolshevik aims

. . . The slogan. 'Down with the Provisional Government,' is an incorrect one at present because, in the absence of a firm (i.e., a class-conscious and organized) majority of the people on the side of the revolutionary proletariat, such a slogan is either an empty
115 phrase or, objectively, it leads to attempts of an adventuristic nature.

We will favour a transfer of power into the hands of the proletarians and semi-proletarians only when the Soviets of Workers' and Soldiers' Deputies adopt our policy and are willing to
120 take this power into their own hands.

The organization of our party, the cohesiveness of the proletarian forces, have clearly proved inadequate during the days of the crisis.

The slogans of the moment are:

1 explain the proletarian line and the proletarian way to end the
125 war

2 criticize the petty bourgeois policy of confidence in and compromise with the government of the capitalists;

3 conduct propaganda and agitation from group to group within each regiment, in each factory, and especially among the most
130 backward masses, such as servants, manual labourers, etc., since the bourgeoisie tried to rely upon them in particular during the days of the crisis;

4 organize, organize, and once more organize the proletariat; in each factory, in each district, in each block.

'On Dual Power: 22 April'. Quoted in Ralph C. Erwood, *Resolutions and Decisions of the Communist Party of the Soviet Union*, vol. I (Toronto, 1974) pp 216–17

Questions

a Outline the contrasting arguments put forward in extract (c) by Chkheidze and Lenin.

b How does the author of this extract show that he is not on the side of Chkheidze?

c In extract (d) why does Lenin demand that no support should be given to the Provisional Government?

d Who does Lenin think should eventually take power? Why can they not take power immediately?

e According to this extract, what were the Bolshevik policies at this time?

f What are Lenin's arguments in extract (e) to explain why the revolution had to move onwards from the initial achievements of February 1917?

g To what extent does extract (f) differ from the ideas put forward in extracts (d) and (e)?

★ *h* Why did Lenin think a second revolution was already taking place when he returned to Russia?

3 The Provisional Government

(a) Government policies

In its present activity the Cabinet will be guided by the following principles:

1. Complete and immediate amnesty for all political and religious cases, including terrorist attacks, military uprisings, agrarian crimes, 5 etc.

2. Freedom of speech, press, union, assembly and strikes, with extension of political liberties to persons in military service within limits consistent with military technical conditions.

3. Abolition of all caste, religious and national discriminations.

10 4. Immediate preparation for the convention of a Constituent Assembly, which will establish the form of adminstration and the constitution of the country, on the basis of general, equal, secret and direct voting.

5. Replacement of the police by a people's militia with an elected 15 administration, subordinated to the organs of local selfgovernment.

6. Elections to the organs of local selfgovernment on the basis of general, direct, equal and secret ballot.

7. The military units which took part in the revolutionary movement are not to be disarmed or removed from Petrograd.

20 8. Along with the maintenance of strict military discipline in the ranks and in military service: elimination for soldiers of all limitations in the enjoyment of the general rights which are granted to all other citizens.

The Provisional Government considers its duty to add that it 25 does not intend to exploit military circumstances for any delay in the realization of the above outlined reforms and measures.

> Quoted in Chamberlain, vol I, op cit, p 432

(b) The Government and the war

(i) The Government of the old regime, of course, could not adopt and share these ideas of the liberating character of the War, of the creation of firm bases for the peaceful co-existence of peoples, of 30 the selfdetermination of oppressed nationalities, etc. But liberated Russia at the present time can speak in a language which is understandable for the leading democracies of contemporary humanity, and it hastens to join its voice to the voices of its Allies. Of course the statements of the Provisional Government, which are

permeated with this new spirit of freed democracy, cannot give
the least reason to think that the revolution which has taken place
has brought after it a weakening of the role of Russia in the general
Allied struggle. Quite on the contrary, the popular aspiration to
carry on the World War to a decisive victory has only become
40 intensified, as a result of everyone's consciousness of the general
responsibility. This aspiration became more real, being concentrated
on a problem that is close to all and immediate: to drive back the
enemy who has penetrated into the territories of our motherland.
(Note of Foreign Minister Milyukov)
(ii) The Provisional Government considers it its right and duty to
45 state that the objective of free Russia is not domination over other
peoples, not depriving them of their national possessions, not
violent seizure of other peoples' territories, but the establishment
of complete peace on the basis of the selfdetermination of nationalities. The Russian people does not attempt to strengthen its external
50 power at the expense of other peoples and does not set as its goal
the enslavement and humiliation of anyone. In the name of the
high principles of justice it has struck off the chains which fettered
the Russian people. But the Russian people will not permit that its
motherland should come out of the Great War humiliated and
55 undermined in its vital resources.
(Note of Provisional Government)
Quoted in ibid, pp 444–5

(c) Kerensky and the war

Late on May 12 I set off for the Southwestern Front. At Kamenets-
Podolsk, General Brusilov's headquarters, a congress of delegates
from all parts of the front was in progress, and I addressed the
meeting on May 14. . . .
60   I could sense the mood of the entire army. I had no doubt that
at that moment the army was facing a temptation which it found
difficult to resist. After three years of bitter suffering, millions of
war-weary soldiers were asking themselves: 'Why should I have to
die now when at home a new, freer life is only just beginning?' . . .
65   No army can afford to start questioning the aim for which it is
fighting. Everything that was happening in the army at that
moment – insubordination, the mutinies, the conversion to Bolshevism of whole units, the endless political meetings, and the mass
desertion – was the natural outcome of the terrible conflict in the
70 mind of each soldier. The men had suddenly found a way of
justifying their weakness, and they were overcome by an almost
unconquerable urge to drop their weapons and flee from the
trenches. To restore their fighting capacity we had to overcome
their animal fear and answer their doubts with the clear and simple
75 truth: You must make the sacrifice to save your country. People

who did not understand the feelings of the soldiers in those crucial months in Russian history, or who spoke to them in patriotic platitudes couched in high-flown language, could not reach their hearts or have any influence on them.

80   My words to the soldiers were: 'It's easy to appeal to exhausted men to throw down their arms and go home, where a new life has begun. But I summon you to battle, to feats of heroism – I summon you not to festivity, but to death; to sacrifice yourselves to save your country!'

    Alexander Kerensky, *The Kerensky Memoirs* (1965) pp 276–7

Questions

a   Summarise the policies of the Provisional Government listed in extract (a).

b   How liberal were these policies?

c   In extract (b), why does the Provisional Government expect Russia to fight more strongly since the tsar has been deposed?

d   According to this extract, what are the war aims of the government?

e   What is Kerensky's explanation in extract (c) for the low morale in the army? What is his way of dealing with it?

(d) An assessment of Kerensky

Kerensky was the victim of the bourgeois hopes which his short-lived success aroused. He was an honest, if not a great man – sincere in spite of his oratorical talents, and, for a man who for four months was worshipped as a god, comparatively modest.
5 From the start he was fighting a hopeless battle, trying to drive back into the trenches a nation which had already finished with the war. Caught between the cross-fires of the Bolshevik Left, which was screaming peace at every street corner and in every trench, and of the Right and of the Allies, who were demanding the
10 restoration of discipline by Tsarist methods, he had no chance. . . .

    Yet for a few weeks it seemed that his oratory might work a miracle and that his ridicuous belief (shared by all the Social-revolutionaries and most of the Liberals) in the commonsense of the Russian people might justify itself. . . .
15 Kerensky held up his hand and plunged straight into his speech. He looked ill and tired. He drew himself up to his full height, as if calling up his last reserves of energy. Then, with an ever-increasing flow of words, he began to expound his gospel of suffering. Nothing that was worth having could be achieved without suffering. Man
20 himself was born into this world in suffering. The greatest of all revolutions in history had begun on the Cross of Calvary. Was it

to be supposed that their own revolution was to be consolidated without suffering? They had a legacy of appalling difficulties left to them by the Tsarist regime: disorganised transport, lack of
25 bread, lack of fuel. Yet the Russian people knew how to suffer. He had just returned from the trenches. He had seen men who had been living for months on end with mud and water up to their knees. Lice crawled over them. For days they had had nothing but a crust of black bread for sustenance. They were without the proper
30 equipment for their self-defence. They had not seen their women-folk for months. Yet they made no complaint. They had promised to do their duty to the end. It was only in St. Petersburg and in Moscow that he heard grumbling. And from whom? From the rich, from those who, in their silks and ornaments of gold, came
35 here today to listen to him in comfort.

Lockart, op cit, pp 177–8

(e) Political parties and the Government

That the passing of all power to the Soviets of Workers' and Soldiers' Deputies in the present period of the Russian Revolution would have considerably weakened its forces, would have prematurely pushed away from it elements which are still able to serve it
40 and would have threatened the Revolution with disaster.

After hearing the explanations of the Comrades Ministers about the general policy of the Provisional Revolutionary Government the All-Russian Congress expresses its full confidence in them and recognises that the direction of this policy corresponded with the
45 interests of the Revolution.

The Congress urges the Provisional Government to carry out more vigorously and logically the democratic platform which it has accepted and especially:

(a) To struggle insistently for the speediest achievement of a
50 general peace without annexations and contributions on the basis of selfdetermination of the peoples;
(b) To carry out the further democratization of the Army and to strengthen its fighting capacity.
(c) To adopt the most energetic measures for combating break-
55 down in the fields of finance, economic life and food supply, with the direct participation of the working masses.
(d) To carry out a systematic and decisive struggle with counter-revolutionary attempts.
. . .
(g) The congress especially demands the convocation at the
60 earliest possible moment of the All-Russian Constituent Assembly.

Social Revolutionary and Menshevik Resolutions to the

(f) A critic on the Government

So they talked and listened, and ran from this bleating gathering
to that baaing crowd, thoroughly delighted with their sheeps'
paradise because they could make as much noise as they liked
65 without interference from the dog. It was exasperating to those
like myself who were not so avid of talk and were eager to be
doing something, but it was understandable as a stage through
which the revolution had to pass. Freedom of speech was a new
toy to them and they had to be allowed to wear it out.
70   Meanwhile, the members of the Provisional Government and
their supporters were tearing their nerves to tatters between frantic
conferences by day to decide what should be done and blustering
performances on the conjurers' platforms in the evening telling the
people how splendid it would all be when they had done it, and
75 how glad they should be to have men like themselves who could
talk so well about when they were going to do it. The majority of
them were completely incompetent, of course, from sheer lack of
experience of political control. There was simply no tradition to
guide them, no machinery even which they could employ. The
80 old bureaucracy was anathema to everybody and was a wolf in the
midst of the sheep waiting a chance to snap.
    The Government, too, was a coalition without a goal. The
parties were mistrustful of one another and without confidence in
themselves. Like the soldiers and the people, they had accomplished
85 their only aim when they had got rid of the Tsar and with the
wind of their opposition to the absolute monarchy out of their sails
they were ships becalmed. The only point they were at all united
on was their will to go ahead with the war.
    Blair and David, op cit, pp 112–13

Questions

a How does the author of extract (d) assess the character of
   Kerensky?
b According to this extract, how did Kerensky try to inspire the
   Russian people?
c Compare the demands of the Social Revolutionaries and Mensheviks in extract (e) and the policies of the Provisional
   Government in extract (a).
* d Why did the Social Revolutionaries and Mensheviks support
      the government?
e What criticisms are levelled against the Provisional Government
   in extract (f)?
* f What problems faced the Provisional Government in the period
      February–June 1917?

IV The Provisional Government (ii) July–October

Introduction

It is very easy to belittle the Provisional Government but in its admittedly brief lifetime it was the most liberal administration that had ever been seen in Russia and with the prospect of full, democratic elections in the months to come. Yet the promise was never fulfilled and the government became increasingly unpopular, saddled as it was with the dismal prospect of a war which continued to go badly for Russia despite the change of government. Naturally, it was those at the top who took the blame for this state of affairs and as almost all political parties were represented in the Provisional Government, their standing suffered severely.

The one group that stood aloof from all this was the Bolshevik Party which was thus able to see a steady growth in its support over the summer months of 1917. Lenin expected the party to be in a position to seize power within a short space of time. The delay was still too long for some. Spontaneous demonstrations, the so-called July Days, began to turn into something potentially more dangerous. Here was a true Marxist mass movement but the Bolsheviks were unsure how to exploit it. After some hesitation, Lenin decided these riots were too premature. The unrest did die down, but it provided an excuse for Kerensky to turn on the Bolshevik Party as a whole. The leaders went into hiding. The Red Guards were disarmed.

The narrow base of support for the Provisional Government was further emphasised by the Kornilov uprising. It also showed the confused nature of politics at that time as this military leader announced that he was marching on Petrograd because Kerensky was dominated by the Bolsheviks. Kornilov's threat had the opposite effect to that which was intended. Kerensky frantically rearmed the Red Guards and the revolt collapsed ignominiously. The Bolsheviks were now back in a strong political position; and if their military power was less sure, they were secure in the knowledge that by October 1917 there would be few ready to die for the Provisional Government in the event of an attempted takeover.

1　The July Days

(a)　A communist version

The political crisis referred to was the demonstration in Petrograd that took place on July 3 and 4 1917; this demonstration was an expression of the profound political crisis then obtaining in Russia.
The setback of the Russian offensive at the front, launched in the
5　interests of the British and French imperialists, the growth of unemployment due to the closure of factories, rising prices and an acute food shortage evoked a storm of indignation among the masses of workers and soldiers over the counter-revolutionary policy of the Provisional Government. On July 3 spontaneous
10　demonstrations broke out, which threatened to turn into an armed uprising against the Provisional Government.

At this time the Bolshevik Party was against an armed uprising because it considered that the revolutionary crisis had not yet matured, that the army and the provinces were not ready to support
15　an uprising in the capital. At a joint meeting of the Central Committee and the Military organisations of the R.S.D.L.P.(B) on July 3, it was decided to refrain from armed action. But the uprising nevertheless began and could not then be stopped.

The Bolsheviks decided to take part in the demonstration on
20　July 4, in order to impart it an organised and peaceful character.

More than 500,000 people took part in the demonstration of July 4, which was conducted under such Bolshevik slogans as 'All power to the Soviets!' The demonstrators sent a 90-man deputation to hand over to the C.E.C. of the Soviets their demand that all
25　power be transferred to the Soviets. But the Socialist-Revolutionary and Menshevik leaders refused to take power into their own hands.

Officer cadets and counter-revolutionary Cossack troops were sent out against this peaceful demonstration of workers and soldiers, on whom they opened fire. Counter-revolutionary military units
30　were recalled from the front to smash the revolutionary movement. Having suppressed the demonstration, the bourgeois Provisional Government continued its policy of repression. Disarming of workers, searches and arrests began. The revolutionary units of the Petrograd garrison were sent to the front; Bolshevik newspapers
35　were banned.

Lenin, *The October Revolution*, op cit, p 386

(b)　A Social Revolutionary's account

First of all, the movement had calmed down during the night; the overwhelming majority of the masses had slept peacefully and shown no desire for action. Secondly, the movement had begun in a dubious way; the Bolshevik Party was far from controlling it,
40　and God knew who was at the head of a great many detachments.

Thirdly, the movement had shown quite clearly its internal feeble-ness and rottenness. The uprising had no striking power, nor any real fitness for battle. The outlook was dubious. Now the chief hope lay in the Kronstadters, whose arrival was expected hourly.
45 But in general – was it worth taking this movement into one's own hands?

It was a question, after all, of the following day, Tuesday July 4th.

This was the first question that confronted Lenin and his comrades
50 that night. And I think it was the only one that demanded an answer. For the second was probably already decided. This was the question of where to lead the movement. This was not a question of concrete fact but of party position. And that had already been determined – a month before. We recall what it reduced itself
55 to: the movement was beginning as a peaceful demonstration, and if it developed adequately it would at a favourable conjuncture pass over into the seizure of power by the Bolshevik Central Committee, which would rule in the name of the Soviet, with the support at the given moment of the majority of the Petersburg proletariat and
60 the active army units. This question was doubtless decided this way now too: a renewal of the debates concerning it was hardly time now, in the smoke of an uprising.

But how was the first point decided: Whether to take over the movement? Speaking concretely this meant: Should they call for a
65 continuation of the 'peaceful demonstration' in the name of the Central Committee of the Party? According to all the evidence this point made the Bolshevik leaders go through tormenting doubts and vacillations the whole night.

In the evening the question was decided positively. Correspond-
70 ing local orders were given. And a corresponding sheet was prepared for the first page of *Pravda*. The Bolsheviks officially and definitely put themselves at the head of the uprising.

But later the mood changed. The lull in the streets and the districts, in connection with the firm course of the Star Chamber,
75 inclined the scales to the opposite side. Irresolution came to the fore. And in this irresolution the Bolsheviks held back once again. The type for the first page of *Pravda* was not only set up, but in the matrix: it had to be cut out of the stereotype machine. The Bolsheviks countermanded their summons to a 'peaceful
80 demonstration'. They declined to continue the movement and stand at its head. . . . On July 4th *Pravda* came out with a yawning blank strip on the first page.

Sukhanov, op cit, pp 438–9

(c) The backlash

On the morning of the fifth I met Lenin. The offensive by the masses had been beaten off. 'Now they will shoot us down, one by one,' said Lenin. 'This is the right time for them.' But he overestimated the opponent – not his venom, but his courage and ability to act. They did not shoot us down one by one, although they were not far from it. Bolsheviks were being beaten down in the street and killed. Military students sacked the Kseshinskaya Palace and the printing-works of the *Pravda*. The whole street in front of the works was littered with manuscripts, and among those destroyed was my pamphlet 'To the Slanders'. The deep reconnaissance of July had been transformed into a one-sided battle. The enemy were easily victorious, because we did not fight. The party was paying dearly for it. Lenin and Zinoviev were in hiding. General arrests, followed by beatings, were the order of the day. Cossacks and military students confiscated the money of those arrested, on the ground that it was 'German money'. Many of our sympathizers and half-friends turned their backs on us. In the Taurïde Palace we were proclaimed counter-revolutionists and were actually put outside the law.

Trotsky, *My Life*, op cit, pp 325–6

(d) Provisional Government weaknesses

At that time it would not have been difficult to suppress the Bolshevist organization completely. Nevertheless, the Soviet did not go so far. It did not even expel the Bolsheviks. Why? Because to take such strong steps against the Left while continuing to compromise with the Right, when General Kornilov was beginning his political demonstrations, meant breaking forever with democracy and openly joining the counterrevolution. To disarm the Bolsheviks and their sympathizers completely was possible only for a government which could win the sympathy of the toiling masses by far-reaching social reforms, by a firm policy in the question of war and peace and by creating radically new conditions for nationalities in Russia. But the government was paralyzed by its alliance with the bourgeois nationalists. It had to counterbalance its concessions to them by equal tolerance of Left-wing extremism. In other words it had to be weak on both fronts.

Chernov, op cit, p 427

(e) A Bolshevik Resolution: 3 August

At the present time state power (in Russia) is, in fact, in the hands of the counter-revolutionary bourgeoisie supported by the military clique. It is precisely this imperialist dictatorship which has carried

120 out and is carrying out . . . the destruction of political liberty, the coercion of the masses, and the ruthless persecution of the internationalist proletariat – while the central institution of the Soviets, the Central Executive Committee, remains totally impotent and inactive.

125 The Soviets, suffering in painful agony, are disintegrating as a result of the fact that they did not at the right time take all the power of the state into their own hands.

The slogan of transferring power to the Soviets, which was advanced during the initial upsurge of the revolution, and propaga-
130 ted by our party, was a slogan of the peaceful development of the revolution, of the painless transfer of power from the bourgeoisie to the workers and peasants, of the petty bourgeoisie's gradual overcoming of its illusions.

At the present time such peaceful development and painless
135 transfer of power to the Soviets has become impossible, since power has in fact already passed into the hands of the counter-revolutionary bourgeoisie.

The correct slogan at the present time can only be the complete liquidation of the dictatorship of the counter-revolutionary bour-
140 geoisie. Only the revolutionary proletariat, on the condition that it is supported by the poorest peasants, has the strength to carry out this task – which is the task of the new revolutionary resurgence.

Quoted in Elwood, op cit, p 254

Questions

a   According to extract (a), how did the protests of the July Days break out and what part did the Bolsheviks play in them?

b   How do documents (a) and (b) differ in their assessments of the Bolsheviks' role in the July Days?

c   What is the purpose, in document (b), of the story of the first page of *Pravda*?

d   According to extract (c), how did the July Days affect the Bolshevik Party?

e   Compare the reasons given in extracts (c) and (d) as to why the Bolsheviks were not treated too harshly.

f   In extract (e), what lessons did the Bolsheviks appear to have learnt from the July Days and how had their tactics changed?

★ g   Using these extracts, and other information known to you, explain why the July Days took place.

2 The Kornilov Uprising

(a) Kornilov's appeal

Russian people.
Our great Motherland is perishing.
The final hour is near.
Compelled to come out openly, I, General Kornilov, declare that
5   the Provisional Government under the pressure of the Bolshevik
majority of the Soviets, acts in full agreement with the plans of the
German General Staff, simultaneously with the impending descent
of hostile forces on the Riga coast, destroys the Army and upsets
the country from within. The painful consciousness of the inevitable
10   destruction of the country commands me at this threatening
moment to summon all Russian people to save the perishing
motherland. Let all in whose breasts beat Russian hearts, all who
believe in God and His churches pray to the Lord God for the
greatest miracle: the salvation of our native land. I, General
15   Kornilov, the son of a cossack peasant, declare to all that personally
I want nothing except the preservation of Great Russia, and I vow
to bring the people, through victory over the enemy, to the
Constituent Assembly, at which the people will itself decide its
own fate and choose its own form of government. I cannot betray
20   Russia into the hands of its historic enemy, the German tribe, and
make the Russian people slaves of the German.
             Quoted in Chamberlain, vol I, op cit, p 462

(b) The role of the Bolsheviks

Meanwhile the government itself began to release us, for the same
reason that it had called in the Bolshevik sailors to guard the Winter
Palace. I went straight from the Kresty to the newly organized
25   committee for the defence of the revolution, where I sat with the
same gentleman who had put me in prison, as an agent of the
Hohenzollerns, and who had not yet withdrawn the accusation
against me. I must candidly confess that the Populists and Mensheviks by their very appearance made one wish that Kornilov
30   might grip them by the scruffs of their necks and shake them in
the air. But this wish was not only irreverent, it was unpolitical.
The Bolsheviks stepped into the harness, and were everywhere in
the first line of the defence. The experience of Kornilov's mutiny
completed that of the July days: once more Kerensky and Co.
35   revealed the fact that they had no forces of their own to back them.
The army that rose against Kornilov was the army-to-be of the
October revolution. We took advantage of the danger to arm the
workers whom Tzereteli had been disarming with such restless
industry.
          Trotsky, *My Life*, op cit, pp 330–1

(c) Propaganda

40 So on the morning of the 28th the echelons of the Savage Division left Dno Station on another line. At 4 o'clock in the afternoon two echelons had got within forty-two versts of Petersburg, where the line was cut and timber-wagons had been overturned. A small reconnaissance detachment left the Kornilov train. From the other
45 direction a special delegation of Muslims and Caucasians specially sent by the Central Ex. Com., went to meet them, to influence their kinsmen in the Savage Division. The delegates suggested that they be taken to the echelons. The detachment willingly agreed, and gave their word of honour that those sent to parley should not
50 be touched. En route they had time to talk, always on the same simple theme.

But a group of Kornilovite officers who had left the train refused to allow the delegation to see the echelons. After long and stormy arguments the delegates had to go back, since it was already after
55 9 o'clock. But they had already done enough to undermine the morale of the detachment: the 'Savages' had been informed of the real state of affairs. Later they told of how they had been lured to Petersburg: first they had been told they were being taken north of Riga to repel the Germans; after Dno they were assured that the
60 Bolsheviks were slaughtering people in Petersburg, and that these traitors had to be repressed. To make things more convincing a provocateur threw a bomb at the echelon not far from Dno, which heightened morale. But simple information made it fall again. After August 28th, while Miliukov and Kornilov were asserting they
65 had all the real power, that real power, in the form of an isolated Corps, was already coming apart at the seams.

Sukhanov, op cit, p 512

(d) Kerensky on the uprising

Thus the armed revolt against the Government began. For two days, while this attempt was being crushed, different 'conciliators' beseiged the Prime Minister, attempting to persuade him to
70 compromise 'as the real force is on the side of Kornilov.' But already on the 29th of August (Old Style) it became evident that the whole of the real force of the country was against Kornilov, and, as had been predicted to him by Kerensky himself some time before, Kornilov found himself in splendid isolation. On the 31st
75 August (Old Style) the rebellion was definitely and bloodlessly suppressed. It was easy to deal with it. Kornilov was not backed by a single important political organization, nor could he rely upon the force of any class. Owing to their political inexperience, Kornilov and those of the officers who were with him mistook for
80 a real force the grumbling of the 'man in the street,' irritated by

the Revolution, but passive by nature, together with the instigation of various adventurers and the promises of support from isolated politicians. The financial help of a certain group of banking-houses artificially exaggerated the dimensions of this movement.

Alexander Kerensky, *The Prelude to Bolshevism: The Kornilov Rebellion* (1919) pp 19–20

(e) The significance of the uprising

85 I must state that, in fact, it was only the 27th of August that made the 25th of October possible. And that is really the great crime, the unredeemable sin against our native country of those naive dreamers, skilful politicians and bold adventurers who undertook to save Russia by means of a 'White General.' In his proclamation
90 'to the Russian people,' General Kornilov, in spite of all evidence to the contrary, states that the Provisional Government acts under the pressure of the Bolshevik majority of the Soviets, etc. Whether Kornilov himself laboured under a delusion, or lied, is of no importance, but there was nothing, nothing whatever, of the kind
95 at the time in the Soviets, which were clearly leaning to the Right. But Kornilov himself proved a remarkable prophet. Almost immediately following his declaration, the Soviets were everywhere actually seized by the Bolsheviks.

Ibid, p 129

(f) The Bolsheviks and Kornilov

On July 3–4 it could have been argued, without violating the truth,
100 that the correct thing to do was to take power, for our enemies would in any case have accused us of insurrection and ruthlessly treated us as rebels. However, to have decided on this account in favour of taking power at that time would have been wrong, because the objective conditions for the victory of the insurrection
105 did not exist.

(1) We still lacked the support of the class which is the vanguard of the revolution.

We still did not have a majority among the workers and soldiers of Petrograd and Moscow. Now we have a majority in both
110 Soviets. It was created solely by the history of July and August, by the experience of the 'ruthless treatment' meted out to the Bolsheviks, and by the experience of the Kornilov revolt.

(2) There was no country-wide revolutionary upsurge at that time. There is now after the Kornilov revolt; the situation in the provinces
115 and assumption of power by the Soviets in many localities prove this.

. . .

(4) Therefore an insurrection on July 3–4 would have been a

mistake; we could not have retained power either physically or politically. We could not have retained it physically even though
120 Petrograd was at times in our hands, because at that time our workers and soldiers would not have fought and died for Petrograd.
. . .

We could not have retained power politically on July 3–4 because, before the Kornilov revolt, the army and the provinces could and would have marched against Petrograd.

Lenin, *Marxism and Insurrection* (Moscow, 1980) pp 11–12

Questions

a In extract (a) what reasons does Kornilov give for launching his rebellion?

★ *b* How accurate an assessment of the state of the Provisional Government is that mapped out by Kornilov in this extract?

c Why do you think that Kornilov includes the line 'I . . . the son of a Cossack peasant' (line 15)?

d Why were the Bolsheviks released, according to extract (b)?

e In extract (c), how and why did the Kornilov advance come to a halt?

f Why did the uprising fail according to Kerensky in extract (d)?

g Compare the assessments of the importance of the Kornilov uprising in extracts (e) and (f).

3   The Bolsheviks and other parties

(a) *Moderate parties*

An article in *Rabochi Put* (*Workers' Way*) about the middle of October, entitled 'The Socialist Ministers', expressing the feeling of the masses of the people against the 'moderate' Socialists:
Here is a list of their services.
5 Tseretelly: disarmed the workmen with the assistance of General Polovtsev, checkmated the revolutionary soldiers, and approved of capital punishment in the army.
Skobeliev: commenced by trying to tax the capitalists 100 per cent of their profits, and finished – and finished by an attempt to dissolve
10 the Workers' Committees in the shops and factories.
Avksentiev: put several hundred peasants in prison, members of the Land Committees, and suppressed dozens of workers' and soldiers' newspapers.
Chernov: signed the 'Imperial' manifesto, ordering the dissolution
15 of the Finnish Diet.
Savinkov: concluded an open alliance with General Kornilov. If this saviour of the country was not able to betray Petrograd, it was due to reasons over which he had no control.

Zarudny: with the sanction of Alexinsky and Kerensky, put some
of the best workers of the Revolution, soldiers and sailors, in
prison.

Nitikin: acted as a vulgar policeman against the railway workers.

Kerensky: it is better not to say anything about him. The list of
his services is too long. . . .

Reed, op cit, p 31

(b) Lenin's view

Either we have to be revolutionary democrats in fact, in which
case we must not fear to take steps towards socialism.

Or we fear to take steps towards socialism, condemn them in
the Plekhanov, Dan or Chernov way, by arguing that our revolution
is a bourgeois revolution, that socialism cannot be 'introduced',
etc., in which case we inevitably sink to the level of Kerensky, i.e.,
we in a reactionary bureaucratic way suppress the 'revolutionary–
democratic' aspirations of the workers and peasants.

There is no middle course.

. . .

Our Socialist-Revolutionaries and Mensheviks approach the
question of socialism in a doctrinaire way, from the standpoint of
a doctrine learnt by heart but poorly understood. They picture
socialism as some remote, unknown and dim future.

But socialism is now gazing at us from all the windows of
modern capitalism; socialism is outlined directly, practically, by
every important measure that constitutes a step forward on the
basis of this modern capitalism.

Lenin, *The Impending Catastrophe and How to Combat it*
(Moscow, 1975) pp 47–8

(c) Famine is approaching

Unavoidable catastrophe is threatening Russia. The railways are
incredibly disorganised and the disorganisation is progressing. The
railways will come to a standstill. The delivery of raw materials
and coal to the factories will cease. The delivery of grain will
cease. The capitalists are deliberately and unremittingly sabotaging
(damaging, stopping, disrupting, hampering) production, hoping
that an unparalleled catastrophe will mean the collapse of the
republic and democracy, and of the Soviets and proletarian and
peasant associations generally, thus facilitating the return to a
monarchy and the restoration of the unlimited power of the
bourgeoisie and the landowners.

The danger of a great catastrophe and of famine is imminent.
All the newspapers have written about this time and again. A
tremendous number of resolutions have been adopted by the parties

and by the Soviets of Workers', Soldiers' and Peasants' Deputies –
resolutions which admit that a catastrophe is unavoidable, that it is
very close, that extreme measures are necessary to combat it, that
'heroic efforts' by the people are necessary to avert ruin, and so
60 on.
 Everybody says this. Everybody admits it. Everybody has
decided it is so. Yet nothing is being done.
  Ibid, p 8

(d) An interview with Trotsky

He went on to speak of the new Government's foreign policy:
'Our first act will be to call for an immediate armistice on all fronts,
65 and a conference of peoples to discuss democratic peace terms. The
quantity of democracy we get in the peace settlement depends on
the quantity of revolutionary response there is in Europe. If we
create here a Government of the Soviets, that will be a powerful
factor for immediate peace in Europe; for this Government will
70 address itself directly and immediately to all peoples, over the heads
of their Governments, proposing an armistice. At the moment of
the conclusion of peace the pressure of the Russian Revolution will
be in the direction of 'no annexations, no indemnities, the right
of self-determination of peoples', and a Federated Republic of
75 Europe. . . .
  Reed, op cit, pp 68–9

Questions

a What are the major criticisms levelled against the ministers
 mentioned in extract (a)?

b Why does Lenin pour scorn on the Social Revolutionaries and
 Mensheviks in extract (b)?

c In extract (c), to whom does Lenin apportion blame for the
 present situation in Russia?

★ *d* How accurate an assessment of the state of Russia in autumn
 1917 is extract (c)?

e According to extract (d), what were the Bolsheviks' aims in
 foreign policy?

★ *f* How would these aims also provide a solution to the peasants'
 demand for land?

(e) Parties: July–October

Comparative Table of the Moscow Municipal Wards Elections of
the 12th October, 1917, showing changes in the various parties

since the Moscow General Municipal Elections of the 8th July, 1917.

Parties	July 1917	%	October 1917	%
Constitutional-Democrats (Cadets)	108,781	16.85%	101,106	26.2%
Social-Revolutionaries	374,885	57.98%	54,374	14.0%
Social-Democrats (Minimalists-Mensheviki)	76,407	11.82%	15,887	4.0%
Social-Democrats (Maximalists-Bolsheviki)	75,409	11.66%	198,320	51.3%
Other Parties	—	1.69%		4.5%
Total Number of Votes	646,568		335,847	

There are some interesting conclusions to be drawn from the above figures. . . .

The failure of the revolution to settle or ameliorate the economic crisis has led to two tendencies: (1) a strengthening of the extremist vote among the workmen and soldiers and (2) an increase of the reactionary or, rather one might say, of the 'reasonable and common-sense' vote among the better-educated town population including a considerable proportion of the more moderate Socialists and also, although it would be rash to state this as a definite fact, among a certain portion of the peasantry.

Secondly, the Cadet Vote, i.e. the vote of the more intellectual and better-educated class has improved considerably. The actual number of Cadet Votes polled, is about the same. When, however, one bears in mind the fact that the people most likely to be deterred from voting are the upper-classes, it is comparatively safe to assume that not only has the Cadet Vote been well maintained but also in reality considerably improved.

Thirdly, the Minimalists or Mensheviki who before the revolution possessed the majority of the workmen's votes have dwindled away into insignificance. This is the party of such men as M. M. Tcheidge, Tseretelli, Prokopovitch and Nikitin. The falling away of the supporters of these leaders explains their fall and the ascendancy of the Bolshevik element in the workmen's and soldier's councils. Fourthly, the failure of the Social-Revolutionary Party at the last elections must be carefully noticed in connection with the recent fall of M. Kerensky and the Provisional Government. At the July elections the Social-Revolutionaries won a complete victory largely on account of the magic influence of M. Kerensky's name and of their land programme. Their failure to bring the land programme into effect and to improve the food question lost them many supporters among the more ignorant section of the

population, while, as far as M. Kerensky is concerned, his supposed complicity in the Korniloff affair lost him as many votes among the more extreme Members of his party as did his weakness in the same affair among the more reactionary element who had at first
50 been induced to support him as the lesser of the two evils.

Fifthly, the Bolshevik vote, which in Petrograd and Moscow is drawn largely from the military element, i.e. a purely floating element, represents an anti-war vote influenced mainly by the economic crisis. In fact, if the Social-Revolutionary and the Social-
55 Democrat Minimalist vote be taken as a more-or-less pro-war vote, one finds that in July at Moscow the pro-war Socialist vote represented some 451,000 votes or roughly 70% of the total voters as against a 12% anti-war or Bolshevik vote. Only three months later, the position had so far changed as to reduce the pro-war
60 Socialist vote to 18% and increased the anti-war Socialist vote to over 50%.

> Public Record Office: FO 371 3000. Enclosure in Mr Lockhart's despatch of 24 November 1917

Questions

a   According to the table in extract (e), how had each party's share of the vote changed between July and October 1917?
b   What are Lockhart's explanations for the change of fortunes of: the Cadets; Mensheviks; Social Revolutionaries?
★ c   Using this extract and other information known to you, explain why the Bolsheviks increased their support so dramatically during this period.

4   Provisional Government Problems

(a) *Army discipline*

> Monday, April 30, 1917.

The forces of anarchy are swelling and raging with the uncontrollable force of an equinoctial tide.

All discipline has vanished in the army. Officers are everywhere
5 being insulted, ragged and − if they object − massacred. It is calculated that more than 1,200,000 deserters are wandering over Russia, filling the stations, storming the carriages, stopping the trains, and thus paralysing all the military and civil transport services. At junctions in particular they seem positively to swarm.
10 A train arrives: they make its occupants get out, take their places and compel the stationmaster to switch the train off in any direction they like. Or it may be a train laden with troops for the front. The men get out at some station, arrange a meeting, confer together for an hour or two, and wind up by demanding to be taken back
15 to their starting point.

> Paléologue, op cit, p 908

(b) Daily life in Petrograd

September and October are the worst months of the Russian year –
especially the Petrograd year. Under dull grey skies, in shortening
20 days, the rain fell drenching, incessant. The mud underfoot was
deep, slippery, and clinging, tracked everywhere by heavy boots,
and worse than usual because of the complete breakdown of the
Municipal administration. Bitter damp winds rushed in from the
Gulf of Finland, and the chill fog rolled through the streets. At
25 night, for motives of economy as well as fear of Zeppelins, the
street-lights were few and far between; in private dwellings and
apartment houses the electricity was turned on from six o'clock
until midnight, with candles forty cents apiece and little kerosene
to be had. It was dark from three in the afternoon to ten in the
30 morning. Robberies and house-breaking increased. In apartment
houses the men took turns at all-night guard duty, armed with
loaded rifles. This was under the Provisional Government.

Week by week food became scarcer. The daily allowance of
bread fell from a pound and a half to a pound, then three-quarters,
35 half, and a quarter-pound. Towards the end there was a week
without any bread at all. Sugar one was entitled to at the rate of
two pounds a month – if one could get it at all, which was seldom.
A bar of chocolate or a pound of tasteless candy cost anywhere
from seven to ten roubles – at least a dollar. There was milk for
40 about half the babies in the city; most hotels and private houses
never saw it for months. In the fruit season apples and pears sold
for a little less than a rouble apiece on the street corner. . . .

Reed, op cit, p 37

Questions

a Why might source (a) be an exaggerated account?
★ b Explain the reference to Zeppelins in extract (b) (line 25).
c What impression does extract (b) give of daily life in Petrograd?

(c) Russian politics

Meanwhile, what of the Duma, the legally elected, representative
assembly which alone could claim to voice the collective will of
the Russian people? Much and heated controversy centres about
that body, apologists of the monarchy assailing it bitterly as a
5 hotbed of treasonable conspiracy, while neutral historians blame
its members severely for the feebleness and indecision of its policy.
Truth is, no one had a clear idea or a political programme, much
less a determined will to assume leadership at a moment when the

mounting passion of the populace created disorders which needed,
above all else, cool heads, alert minds, and eyes that saw something
more relevant to Russia's future than the welcome vision of a
toppling throne, burning police stations, and jail deliveries. Everyone foresaw the Revolution, and no one prepared for it. Gutchkov's
frank admission is the key to the kaleidoscopic variations that are
to follow: 'The destruction of old forms of life was faster than the
creation of new forms to replace them.'

Walsh, op cit, p 201

(d) Political freedom

The change was at the outset wholly destructive, but it was too
great to be contained, and now that passions were kindled it made
the whole of the past obsolete in a day. Though no one seemed to
notice it, the substance of what happened every day was that more
and more of the relics of the past were swept away. The police
were abolished because they had fired on the people; the army
broke up because its allegiance, and very soon its discipline, were
gone. The local authorities were swept away in the rush. What
was there left to govern with? Guchkov, who had himself planned
an abortive plot against the sovereign, had said that the power
would go after the revolution to those who made it. The power,
then, was now with the mob, and who could curb the mob? Not
a Provisional Government, to call it by the modest name which it
took. Every day it became more out of date, and from the first
day of its agitated existence there was a Soviet representing the
revolted armed force of the capital sitting in the Duma's own
debating hall.

Pares, *Russia*, op cit, pp 100–1

(e) Criticism with hindsight

What it is important to realise is that from the first the revolution
was a revolution of the people. From the first moment neither the
Duma nor the intelligentzia had any control of the situation.
Secondly, the revolution was a revolution for land, bread and
peace – but, above all, for peace. There was only one way to save
Russia from going Bolshevik. That was to allow her to make peace.
It was because he would not make peace that Kerensky went under.
It was solely because he promised to stop the war that Lenin came
to the top. It will be objected that Kerensky ought to have shot
both Lenin and Trotsky. The soldiers, who argue in this way,
always ignore the psychological premises. The old regime having
broken down, the type of leader (i.e. a Kerensky) whom the first
revolution threw up was bound to be a man who would not shoot
his opponents. It was the first stage of a natural process. Secondly,

even if Kerensky had shot Lenin and Trotsky, some other anti-war
leader would have taken their place and would have won through
50 on his anti-war programme.

Lockhart, op cit, p 171

(f) The leaders of the Provisional Government

The tragedy of the position of Russia at the end of the summer of
1917 lay precisely in its not having yet attained such political
maturity as would have afforded to its leading political circles the
possibility of realizing to the very end and of carrying through the
55 only system of organizing the State authority which alone could
still have stopped the threatening process of the collapse of the
State, which had commenced together with the world-war, viz.
the system of coalition between all the political parties that were
holding to the idea of a State, in order to create a common national
60 Government. The condition of the economic organism and of the
technical apparatus of the State had made it impossible to govern
the country during war by the strength of any minority whatsoever,
which is always and inevitably reduced to applying political terror
as the sole means of keeping the majority in subjection.
65   Unfortunately, the leading political circles, which could not help
recognizing that the coalition was indispensable, did not support it
actively and fairly. They were only rather afraid to take upon
themselves the political responsibility for the formal collapse of
that system, while in their own mind they were waiting for a
70 'saviour,' whom some expected from the Right and others from
the Left.

Kerensky, *The Prelude to Bolshevism*, op cit, pp 280–1

Questions

a Compare extracts (c) and (d) in their criticisms of the Provisional
    Government?
★ b How free was Russia in the period February–October 1917?
c According to extract (e), why did Kerensky not execute Lenin
    and Trotsky?
★ d 'It was solely because he promised to stop the war that Lenin
    came to the top' (lines 41–2). Discuss.
e In extract (f), who does Kerensky blame for the downfall of
    the government?
★ f Why did the Provisional Government fall from power?

V The October Revolution

Introduction

The October Revolution was far from being the sudden and bloody event that is usually portrayed. Many expected it, especially after two dissenting voices in the Bolshevik leadership publicly voiced reservations about its timing in newspapers prior to the event. The actual revolution was a minor affair without heroics. The Bolsheviks seized key points in Petrograd with little effort and the Kronstadt sailors and the Red Guards had little fighting to do. By early evening only the Winter Palace was left to be captured and while the Bolshevik troops moved against it, night life in Petrograd continued as usual. The palace surrendered with little bloodshed although some controversy remains over the behaviour of the Bolshevik troops once the defending forces had surrendered.

Most of the Provisional Government were arrested on the spot. Kerensky himself escaped to the front where according to Bolshevik mythology he now became a counter–revolutionary leader. Few troops supported him, however, and his advance stopped abruptly outside Petrograd. Kerensky fled again, this time for good. No one cared enough to fight for him.

It was much the same for other organs of government. The Second Congress of Soviets was meeting on the evening of the takeover. The Bolsheviks already held a majority of seats there so that with the announcement of the fall of the Provisional Government the only recourse the other parties had was to walk out. This the Social Revolutionaries and Mensheviks did, leaving behind the Bolsheviks and more radical, or Left, Social Revolution-aries.

There was one other body, the Constituent Assembly. The Bolsheviks had supported the elections in summer 1917 when they were seeking any and all gains but once they had seized power the Assembly became an irrelevancy.

It was too late to cancel the elections and the results were not pleasing. The Bolsheviks and Left Social Revolutionaries failed to achieve a majority so they walked out this time. The difference was that they had the muscle to get their way. Troops closed down the Assembly thus ending the one and only day of democratic government in Russia.

So far, so good; but appearances can be deceptive. The Bolsheviks had found it relatively easy to close down rival governing bodies as their opponents were divided and lacked force. There were many opponents, though, and once the Bolsheviks began to put their own policies into practice there would be more time and reason for the opposition forces to coalesce.

1 The Takeover

(a) Lenin's demands

The Bolsheviks, having obtained a majority in the Soviets of Workers' and Soldiers' Deputies of both capitals, can and must take state power into their own hands.

5 They can because the active majority of revolutionary elements in the two chief cities is large enough to carry the people with it, to overcome the opponent's resistance, to smash him and to gain and retain power. For the Bolsheviks, by immediately proposing a democratic peace, by immediately giving the land to the peasants and by re-establishing the democratic institutions and liberties

10 which have been mangled and shattered by Kerensky, will form a government which nobody will be able to overthrow.
. . .

Why must the Bolsheviks assume power at this very moment?

Because the impending surrender of Petrograd will make our chances a hundred times less favourable.

15 And it is not in our power to prevent the surrender of Petrograd while the army is headed by Kerensky and Co.

Nor can we 'wait' for the Constituent Assembly, for by surrendering Petrograd Kerensky and Co. can always frustrate its convocation. Our Party alone, on taking power, can secure the Constituent

20 Assembly's convocation; it will then accuse the other parties of procrastination and will be able to substantiate its accusations.

The people are tired of the waverings of the Mensheviks and Socialist-Revolutionaries. It is only our victory in the metropolitan cities that will carry the peasants with us.
. . .

25 It would be naive to wait for a 'formal' majority for the Bolsheviks. No revolution ever waits for that. Kerensky and Co. are not waiting either, and are preparing to surrender Petrograd.
. . .

History will not forgive us if we do not assume power now.

The Bolsheviks must assume power (12–14 September 1917)
Reprinted in Lenin, *Marxism and Insurrection*, op cit, pp 7–9.

(b) Bolshevik worries

Nevsky: As a representative of the military organization I must call
30 your attention to a number of difficulties confronting us. The
military organization suddenly began to move to the Right. . . .
Instead of the village turning away from us it has only begun to
come to us. We receive information from numerous places that the
Bolsheviks are beginning to become popular. The decisive factor
35 in the revolution is, of course, the working class. . . . But we must
not on that account neglect the spirit of the peasant masses; if we
do we shall not win the victory. In quite a number of gubernias
. . . the peasants say that in case of an insurrection they will not
give us any bread. Absolutely nothing has been done to stir up the
40 village. An armed uprising of the proletariat here in Petersburg is
a feasible thing. The whole garrison will come out at the call of
the Soviet. . . . But we cannot confine the insurrection to
Petersburg. How will Moscow and the provinces react to this? Can
the Central Committee give us the assurance that Russia as a whole
45 will support us? We all realize that the moment is ripe. But are we
ready? Have we the majority which will guarantee freedom? From
the report it is quite clear that we are not ready, and the question
stands thus: If we should come out, we shall find ourselves isolated
from the rest of Russia. We have no data concerning the situation
50 on the railroads. And are you sure that the 5th Army will not be
sent against us?

> Report from Rank and File of the Bolshevik Party, 28
> October 1917. Quoted in Bunyan and Fisher, op cit, pp
> 70–1

(c) Kerensky rallies support

Now having documentary proof of the incipient revolt, I went
straight to the meeting of the Council of the Republic at 11 a.m.
on October 24, and asked the chairman, Avksentiev, to allow me
55 to speak at once.
After I had spoken for some time, Konovalov approached me
and handed me a note. There was a long pause while I read it, and
then I continued:
'I have just been given a copy of the document which is now
60 being illegally circulated to army units. It reads: "The Petrograd
Soviet is in danger. You are to instruct the regiments to stand by
for further orders. Delay or refusal to obey orders will be considered
treachery to the Revolution. Signed, on behalf of the chairman (of
the Revolutionary Committee), Podvoisky. Secretary Antonov."
65 [Cries of "Traitors!" from the Right.] And so, at the present
moment, the capital is in what is termed in legal language a state
of revolt. We are faced with an attempt to incite the mob against

the existing order, to thwart the plan for a Constituent Assembly
[cries of "Hear, hear!" from the Center and Right], and to lay open
70   the front lines to the armies of Kaiser Wilhelm. [Cries of "Hear,
hear!" from the Right and Center; from the Left, jeering and shouts
of "That's enough!"] I use the term "mob" because the whole of
the democratic movement and its Central Executive Committee,
all the army organizations, and everything that Russia is justly
75   proud of – the reason, conscience, and honour of the great Russian
democracy – protest against it [stormy applause from all the
benches, except the Menshevik Internationalists] . . . . Let it be
understood that the objective danger of this uprising lies not so
much in the possibility that the movement, just as in July, may act
80   as a signal for the Germans to launch a new attack against our
frontiers and may result in a new attempt, even more serious than
Kornilov's attempt.'
              Kerensky, *Memoirs*, op cit, p 434

Questions

a   According to extract (a), why should the Bolsheviks take power
    at this time?
b   In this extract, how will the Bolsheviks be able to retain power
    once they have seized it?
c   What worries are put forward by the speaker in extract (b)?
d   How does Kerensky try to rally support in extract (c)? How
    accurate are his assertions?

(d) The cruiser Aurora

The cruiser 'Aurora' had been under repairs at the Franco-Russian
yards and was supposed to leave Petrograd on November 4 to try
out its new machinery. But in view of the approaching Second
Congress of Soviets, the Tsentrobalt issued an order postponing
5   our departure indefinitely. The sailors of the 'Aurora' were told
they would have to take an active part in the defence of the Soviet
Congress, and, possibly, in an uprising. On November 6 the
Military Revolutionary Committee appointed me commissar of the
cruiser 'Aurora'. A special meeting of the (sailors') committee was
10   called in the presence of the commander and other officers. I briefly
explained the instruction I had received, saying that I was going to
execute all orders of the Military Revolutionary Committee . . .
regardless of the views of the commanding officers. In the evening
(November 6) instructions were received from the Military Revolu-
15   tionary Committee to reopen traffic on the Nikolaevsky
Bridge. . . . It was necessary to move the ship closer to the bridge,
and I gave orders to get up steam . . . and weigh anchor. . . .
      The commander refused to pilot the ship on the pretext that the

'Aurora' would not be able to move on the Neva. I gave orders to
20 take soundings in the channel of the Neva, which showed that the
cruiser could pass quite easily. . . .

At 3.30 a.m. the ship cast anchor near the Nikolaevsky Bridge.
We worked all day, November 7, to bring the ship in fighting
order. . . . Toward evening we received orders from the Military
25 Revolutionary Committee to fire a few blank shots upon receiving
a signal from Peter and Paul Fortress and, if necessary, to shell (the
Winter Palace) with shrapnel. There was no occasion, however,
for the latter, as the Winter Palace soon surrendered. . . .

Report of the Commissar of the cruiser *Aurora*. Printed in
Bunyan and Fisher, op cit, pp 70–1

(e) *The fall of the Winter Palace*

Towards five o'clock on Wednesday the Soviet, which has become
30 master of the whole city, began to isolate the Winter Palace, where
practically the whole of the Government remained. Detachments
occupied all routes giving access to the Palace. Barricades were
erected haphazard, made of logs taken from neighbouring wood
depots, and planks from works under construction.

35 Traffic was gradually stopped, and in the area thus isolated only
troops, armoured cars, and two anti-aircraft guns placed near the
police headquarters on the Nevsky Prospekt remained. Trams were
stopped on this part of the route, but a short distance beyond they
are running as usual, and the ordinary service will be maintained.
40 The disturbances which the actions of the Committee have occa-
sioned are therefore purely local and temporary. Ordinary life is
going on with almost a tinge of indifference.

. . .

First a detachment of troops attempted to approach the Palace
along Millionnay Street, but the machine-gun fire of its defenders
45 stopped it. Owing to the resistance of the guards of the Palace,
which was being defended, as already reported, by officer cadets,
and a women's battalion, two destroyers anchored in the Neva
fired four shells. At the same time armoured cars from the portico
of Morskaya Street, leading into Palace Square, also shelled the
50 building. Firing ensued in which machine-guns rattled intermit-
tently.

. . .

Fighting continued in the vicinity of the Palace. The guns of the
warships and armoured cars continued to fire at intervals until
nearly one o'clock in the morning. During the evening four
55 destroyers, a minelayer, and several minesweepers with landing
forces were brought from Helsingfors and took part in operations
against the Palace. Finally, about 2 a.m., the forces of the Soviet
succeeded in entering the Palace.

While rifle and artillery fire was continuing in the vicinity of the
60 former Imperial Palace a performance was given as usual at the
Orodny Dom, where a large audience assembled to hear M.
Chaliapine, a popular singer.

> *Manchester Guardian*, 10 November 1917. Reprinted 3
> November 1987.

(f) Another view

Czardom broke down under the strain of a war twice as big as the
one in which it had already failed. The Czar was less cruel than
65 feckless, and the Provisional Government in turn proved too
feckless to effect transition into anything but nightmare. It was
symbolical that the Winter Palace fell not to the heroism of
revolutionaries or the blank cartridges of the cruiser Aurora but to
someone's oversight in leaving the back-door open.

> Lord Vansittart, *The Mist Procession* (1958) p 169

(g) Bolshevik behaviour (i)

70 Gradually the Bolsheviks forced an entry and invaded the Palace.
On their way they pillaged every room they entered. The Ministers
retired from one room to another until at last they were arrested
and conveyed to the fortress.

The Palace was pillaged and devastated from top to bottom by
75 the Bolsheviks' armed mob, as though by a horde of barbarians.
All the State papers were destroyed. Priceless pictures were ripped
from their frames by bayonets. Several hundred carefully packed
boxes of rare plate and china, which Kerensky had exerted himself
to preserve, were broken open and the contents smashed or carried
80 off.

The library of Alexander III, the doors of which we had locked
and sealed, and which we never entered, was forced open and
ransacked, books and manuscripts burnt and destroyed. . . .

The colossal crystal lustre, with its artfully concealed music, was
85 smashed to atoms. Desks, pictures, ornaments – everything was
destroyed. I will refrain from describing the hideous scenes which
took place in the wine cellars, and the fate to which some of the
captured women soldiers were submitted.

Such was the inaugural ceremony of the Bolshevik regime.

> Reprinted *Guardian*, 3 November 1987.

(h) Bolshevik behaviour (ii)

90 Carried along by the eager wave of men we were swept into the
right-hand entrance, opening into a great bare vaulted room, the
cellar of the east wing, from which issued a maze of corridors and

staircases. A number of huge packaging cases stood about, and upon these the Red Guards and soldiers fell furiously, battering
95 them open with the butts of their rifles, and pulling out carpets, curtains, linen, porcelain, plates, glass-ware. . . . One man went strutting around with a bronze clock perched on his shoulder; another found a plume of ostrich feathers, which he stuck in his hat. The looting was just beginning when somebody cried,
100 'Comrades! Don't take anything. This is the property of the People!' Immediately twenty voices were crying, 'Stop! Put everything back! Don't take anything! Property of the People!' Many hands dragged the spoilers down. Damask and tapestry were snatched from the arms of those who had them; two men took away the
105 bronze clock. Roughly and hastily the things were crammed back in their cases, and self-appointed sentinels stood guard. It was all utterly spontaneous. . . .

I do not mean to maintain that there was no looting in the Winter Palace. Both after and before the Winter Palace fell there was
110 considerable pilfering. The statement of the Socialist Revolutionary paper *Narod*, and of members of the City Duma, to the effect that precious objects to the value of 500,000,000 roubles had been stolen, was, however, a gross exaggeration.

The most important art treasures of the Palace – paintings,
115 statues, tapestries, rare porcelains, and armouries – had been transferred to Moscow during the month of September; and they were still in good order in the basement of the Imperial Palace there, ten days after the capture of the Kremlin by Bolshevik troops. I can personally testify to this. . . .
120 Individuals, however, especially the general public, which was allowed to circulate freely through the Winter Palace for several days after its capture, made away with table silver, clocks, bedding, mirrors, and some odd vases of valuable porcelain and semi-precious stones, to the value of about 50,000 dollars.
125 The Soviet Government immediately created a special commission, composed of artists and archaeologists, to recover the stolen objects.

About half the loot was recovered, some of it in the baggage of foreigners leaving Russia.
130 Immediately following the taking of the Winter Palace all sorts of sensational stories were published in the anti-Bolshevik press, and told in the City Duma, about the fate of the Women's Battalion defending the Palace. It was said that some of the girl-soldiers had been thrown from the windows into the street, most of the rest
135 had been violated, and many had committed suicide as a result of the horrors they had gone through.

The City of Duma appointed a commission to investigate the matter. On 16 November the commission returned from Levashovo, headquarters of the Women's Battalion. Madame

140 Tyrkova reported that the girls had been at first taken to the
barracks of the Pavlovksy Regiment, and that there some of them
had been badly treated; but at present most of them were at
Levashovo, and the rest scattered about the city in private houses.
Dr. Mandelbaum, another of the commission, testified dryly that
145 none of the women had been thrown out of the windows of the
Winter Palace, that none were wounded, that three had been
violated, and that one had committed suicide, leaving a note which
said that she had been 'disappointed in her ideals'.

Reed, op cit, pp 188, 304–5

Questions

*   *a* In extract (d), what is a commissar? Explain the relationship
between the commissar and the commander of the *Aurora*.

    b How widespread was the fighting in Petrograd according to
extract (e)?

    c Compare the accounts given in extract (d), (e) and (f) concerning
the attack on the Winter Palace. How do they differ?

*   *d* Extracts (g) and (h) describe the looting of the Winter Palace
and the treatment of the women soldiers there. Why do they
reach different conclusions?

2 Taking Control

(a) Lenin on the Bolshevik takeover

On the basis of the returns of the Constituent Assembly elections
we have studied the three conditions which determined the victory
of Bolshevism: (1) an overwhelming majority among the Proletariat; (2) almost half of the armed forces; (3) an overwhelming
5 superiority of forces at the decisive moment at the decisive points,
namely: in Petrograd and Moscow and on the war fronts near the
centre.

But these conditions could have ensured only a very short-lived
and unstable victory had the Bolsheviks been unable to win to their
10 side the majority of the non-proletarian working masses, to win
them from the Socialist-Revolutionaries and the other petty-
bourgeois parties.

That is the main thing. . . .

The bourgeoisie has used state power as an instrument of the
15 capitalist class against the proletariat, against all the working people.
That has been the case in the most democratic bourgeois republics.
Only the betrayers of Marxism have 'forgotten' this.

The proletariat must (after mustering sufficiently strong political
and military 'striking forces') overthrow the bourgeoisie, take state
20 power from it in order to use that instrument for its class aims.

What are the class aims of the proletariat?

Suppress the resistance of the bourgeoisie;

Neutralise the peasantry and, if possible, win them over – at any rate the majority of the labouring, non-exploiting section – to the
25 side of the proletariat;

Organise large-scale machine production, using factories, and means of production in general, expropriated from the bourgeoisie;

Organise socialism on the ruins of capitalism.

> The Constituent Assembly Elections, December 1919. Reprinted in Lenin, *The October Revolution*, op cit, pp 464–5

(b) Initial Bolshevik plans

The Second All-Russia Congress of Soviets of Workers' and
30 Soldiers' Deputies has opened.

Backed by the will of the vast majority of the workers, soldiers and peasants, backed by the victorious uprising of the workers and the garrison which has taken place in Petrograd, the congress takes power into its own hands.
35 The Provisional Government has been overthrown. The majority of the members of the Provisional Government have already been arrested.

The Soviet Government will propose an immediate democratic peace to all the nations and an immediate armistice on all fronts. It
40 will secure the transfer of the land of the landed proprietors, the crown and the monastries to the peasant committees without compensation; it will protect the rights of the soldiers by introducing complete democracy in the army; it will establish workers' control over production; it will ensure the convocation of the Constituent
45 Assembly at the time appointed; it will see to it that bread is supplied to the cities and prime necessities to the villages; it will guarantee all the nations inhabiting Russia the genuine right to self-determination.

The congress decrees: all power in the localities shall pass to the
50 Soviets of Workers', Soldiers' and Peasants' Deputies, which must guarantee genuine revolutionary order.

The congress calls upon the soldiers in the trenches to be vigilant and firm. The Congress of Soviets is convinced that the revolutionary army will be able to defend the revolution against
55 all attacks of imperialism until such time as the new government succeeds in concluding a democratic peace, which it will propose directly to all peoples. The new government will do everything to fully supply the revolutionary army by means of a determined policy of requisitions and taxation of the propertied classes, and
60 also will improve the condition of soldiers' families.

The Kornilov men – Kerensky, Kaledin and others – are attempting to bring troops against Petrograd. Several detachments,

whom Kerensky had moved by deceiving them, have come over
to the side of the insurgent people.

65   Soldiers, actively resist Kerensky the Kornilovite! Be on your
guard!

Railwaymen, hold up all troop trains dispatched by Kerensky
against Petrograd!

Soldiers, workers in factory and office, the fate of the revolution
70 and the fate of the democratic peace is in your hands!

Long live the revolution!

The Second Congress of Soviets, 25–6 October 1917.

Reprinted in Lenin, *The October Revolution*, op cit, pp 20–1

(c) Trotsky at the Congress of Soviets

The insurrection of the masses stands in no need of justification.
What is taking place is not a conspiracy but an insurrection. We
molded the revolutionary will of the Petrograd workers and
75 soldiers. . . . The masses gathered under our banner, and our
insurrection was victorious. But what do they (the other socialists)
offer us? . . . To give up our victory, to compromise, and to
negotiate – with whom? With whom shall we negotiate? With
those miserable cliques which have left the Congress or with those
80 who still remain? But we saw how strong those cliques were?
There is no one left in Russia to follow them. And millions of
workers and peasants are asked to negotiate with them on equal
terms. No, an agreement will not do now. To those who have left
us and to those proposing negotiations we must say: You are a
85 mere handful, miserable, bankrupt; your role is finished, and you
may go where you belong – to the garbage heap of history!

Quoted in Bunyan and Fisher, op cit, p 113

Questions

a   What reasons does Lenin give in extract (a) for the Bolsheviks'
takeover of power?

b   What were the Bolsheviks' initial policies according to extracts
(a) and (b)?

★ c   Explain the reference in extract (b) to 'Kerensky the Kornilovite'
(line 65).

★ d   What does Trotsky mean in extract (c) by the line 'What is
taking place is not a conspiracy but an insurrection' (line 73)?

e   According to this extract, why were the other political parties
destined for 'the garbage heap of history' (line 86)?

(d) Kerensky and counter-revolution

It is now possible to give some account of what happened at and
around Gatchina during the few days preceding November 13.

Kerensky appears to have collected some 3,000 Cossacks with a few guns who, so long as they advanced, met with little or no resistance. Unfortunately for him, he decided to attempt conciliation, with the inevitable result that the two parties began fraternising. This process was completed by the night of November 12–13 when the Cossacks decided to surrender Kerensky to the Bolsheviks. He had, however, disappeared in the interval – disguised, it is believed, as a sailor and is still at large. His flight deprived him of the support of the few who remained true to him and it is safe to say that there is no public man in Russia who has, at this moment, fewer adherents than the late Prime Minister, whose popularity five months ago was unbounded.

Public Record Office: Foreign Office Summary of Recent Events: FO 371 3000

(e) The takeover elsewhere

In Moscow the Bolsheviks had a harder struggle than at Petrograd. Hostilities began on November 9th, when the Junkers (Officers' Training Corps) took the Kremlin, and lasted the best part of a week. Artillery was freely and wildly used, and the most alarming reports reached Petrograd as to the destruction and pillage. As a matter of fact, the destruction, though serious, did not include any building of historical importance and the pillage was imaginary. It is believed that there were some 7,000 casualties in all. Order is now restored, but the banks are forbidden to pay more than 150 roubles to any one person per week.

At Kiev there was a good deal of fighting between the Ukraine regiments and the Bolsheviks on the one hand and the Junkers, Cossacks and a few officers on the other. The former gained the upper hand and the Ukraine has declared its autonomy but not, apparently, its independence. The Provinces of Podolia and Volhynia, which are within the Ukraine limits, are described as being pillaged from end to end by bands of deserters.

In Odessa, things appear to have passed off quietly and Rumcherod, the joint committee of the Roumanian Front, the Black Sea Fleet and the Odessa district has declared for a coalition Socialist Government.

There is no reliable news from the Cossack country, but General Kaledin is believed to be at Novo Cherkask, and General Alexeleff and Mr. Rodzianko to be with him. It is highly improbable that the Cossacks will do more than maintain the independence of their country.

Although the air is thick with rumours of violence and pillage in the provinces, exaggeration is so rife that it is impossible to sift the truth.

Ibid.

a Why did Kerensky's counterattack fail, according to extract (d)?
b In extract (e), why did the capture of Moscow take longer than that of Petrograd?
★ *c* Why is much of the information suspect in extract (e)?

3 The Constituent Assembly

(a) Bolshevik strengths

The results of work were seen in, among other things the votes polled in the Constituent Assembly elections in November 1917, in which, in Russia, the armed forces also participated.

5 In the two chief cities, in the two principal commercial and industrial centres of Russia, the Bolsheviks had an overwhelming, decisive superiority of forces. Here our forces were nearly four times as great as those of the Socialist-Revolutionaries. We had here more than the Socialist-Revolutionaries and Cadets put together.

10 Moreover, our adversaries were split up, for the 'coalition' of the Cadets with the Socialist-Revolutionaries and Mensheviks (in Petrograd and Moscow the Mensheviks polled only 3 per cent of the votes) was utterly discredited among the working people.

Number of Votes Polled in the Constituent Assembly Elections, November 1917 (thousands)

Army and Navy Units	S.R.s	Bolsheviks	Cadets	National and other groups	TOTAL
Northern Front	240.0	480.0	?	60.0	780.0
Western	180.6	653.4	16.7	152.2	976.0
South–Western	402.9	300.1	13.7	290.6	1007.4
Rumanian Front	679.4	167.0	21.4	260.7	1128.6
Caucasian	360.0	60.0	?	—	420.0
Baltic Fleet	—	(120.0)	—	—	(120.0)
Black Sea Fleet	22.2	10.8	—	19.5	52.5
Total	1885.1	1671.3	51.8	756.0	4364.5
		(120.0)	(+)?		(120.0)
		1791.3			(+)?

Summary: the Socialist-Revolutionaries polled 1,885,100 votes, the Bolsheviks polled 1,671,300 votes. If to the latter we add the 120,000 votes (approximately) polled in the Baltic Fleet, the total votes polled by the Bolsheviks will be 1,791,300.

30   The Bolsheviks, therefore, polled a little less than the Socialist-
Revolutionaries.
      And so, by October–November 1917, the armed forces were
half Bolshevik.
      If that had not been the case we could not have been victorious.
35   If we leave out the Caucasian Front, the Bolsheviks obtained on
the whole a majority over the Socialist-Revolutionaries. And if we
take the Northern and Western fronts, the votes polled by the
Bolsheviks will amount to over one million, compared with 420,000
votes polled by the Socialist-Revolutionaries.
40   Thus, in the armed forces, too, the Bolsheviks already had a
political 'striking force', by November 1917, which ensured them
an overwhelming superiority of forces at the decisive point at the
decisive moment. Resistance on the part of the armed forces to the
October Revolution of the proletariat, to the winning of political
45   power by the proletariat, was entirely out of the question, consider-
ing that the Bolsheviks had an enormous majority of the Northern
and Western fronts, far removed from the centre, the Bolsheviks
had the time and opportunity to win the peasants away from the
Socialist-Revolutionary Party.
      The Constituent Assembly Election. Published in Lenin,
      October Revolution, op cit, pp 258–60

(b) A critic on the Bolsheviks

50   If Lenin failed to get a majority in the Constituent, it was certainly
not for the want of trying. Among an electorate the greater part of
which could not read, and practically the whole of which was
completely in the dark as to the relations of the various parties to
the issues at stake, honesty was probably the worst of all policies;
55   and that is no doubt one of the reasons why the Cadets, who had
always prided themselves on the purity of their tactics, secured
only fifteen seats out of a total of 800. The Bolsheviks, on the other
hand, carried to its logical extreme the principle that the end justifies
the means, and were absolutely unembarrassed by any scruples.
60   The work of hocussing the electors was rendered easier by the
complexity of the proportional system and the multiplicity of the
programmes placed before the country. In Petrograd no fewer than
nineteen different lists of candidates were put forward. Most of
them came from parties which never had played, and never will
65   play, any perceptible part in Russian politics – the Christian
Democrats, the Universalist-Socialists, the Bloc of Ukraine and
Hebrew Socialists, the League for the Development of the Nation,
the Orthodox Parishioners, the Women's League of Help for the
Fatherland, the Federation of Workmen, Soldiers and Peasants, and
70   so on. In the provinces, the bewildered peasant was not as a rule
called upon to decide between so many claimants to his confidence;

but cases were numerous in which ten or twelve lists were put into his hands. His ignorance of the fundamental principle of democratic franchise was shown by entire villages deciding at public meetings in favour of one particular party, and then appointing committees to see that all the electors voted accordingly.

Wilcox, op cit, pp 280–1

(c) A Bolshevik statement

The present composition of the Constituent Assembly is largely due to the interrelation of political forces at work before the great November Revolution. The counter-revolutionary majority of the Constituent Assembly . . . [shouts and protests on the Right] was elected on the basis of antiquated party lists and represents yesterday's point of view. [That Majority] is attempting, nevertheless, to block the progress of the workers' and peasants' movement. [Voices from the Right: 'Nonsense!' Applause from the public.] Today's proceedings have made it quite clear that the Socialist-Revolutionists of the Right follow the tactics of Kerensky and feed the people on words, openly promising this and that but underhandedly fighting against the Soviets of Workers, Peasants, and Soldiers, against socialistic measures, against the transfer, without compensation, of the land and implements to the peasants [shouts: 'It is a lie!' Applause from the public], against the nationalization of banks, against repudiation of state debts. [Shouts: 'Idiot!' Applause from the public.] . . .

We do not intend to shield the enemies of the people in their criminal acts, and we hereby . . . withdraw from this Constituent Assembly [shouts of applause from the public] so as to leave it to the Soviet Government to decide finally what attitude it shall take toward the counter-revolutionary section of the Constituent Assembly. [Shouts: 'Pogrom makers!' Applause from the public.]

Quoted in Bunyan and Fisher, op cit, pp 376–7

(d) Lenin dissolves the Constituent Assembly

Those who point out that we are now 'dissolving' the Constituent Assembly although at one time we defended it are not displaying a grain of sense, but are merely uttering pompous and meaningless phrases. At one time, we considered the Constituent Assembly to be better than tsarism and the republic of Kerensky with their famous organs of power; but as the Soviets emerged, they, being revolutionary organisations of the whole people, naturally became incomparably superior to any parliament in the world, a fact that I emphasised as far back as last April. By completely smashing bourgeois and landed property and by facilitating the final upheaval which is sweeping away all traces of the bourgeois system, the

Soviets impelled us on to the path that has led the people to organise their own lives. . . .

Our cry was, All power to the Soviets; it is for this we are fighting. The people wanted the Constituent Assembly summoned
115 and we summoned it. But they sensed immediately what this famous Constituent Assembly really was. And now we have carried out the will of the people, which is – All power to the Soviets. As for the saboteurs, we shall crush them. When I came from Smolny, that fount of life and vigour, to the Taurida Palace, I felt as though
120 I were in the company of corpses and lifeless mummies.

Reprinted in Lenin, *The October Revolution*, op cit, pp 48–50

Questions

★ *a* In extract (a), where were the Bolsheviks strongest and why?
   b How does this extract try to play down the fact that in overall terms the Social Revolutionaries polled more votes?
   c How is extract (b) critical of the Bolsheviks?
   d Compare the reasons given in extracts (c) and (d) for the dissolution of the Constituent Assembly.
   e Extract (c) was printed in an American book of the 1930s. Extract (d) comes from an edition of Lenin's works reprinted in the 1970s. What is included in extract (c) but omitted from extract (d), and why?

VI Civil War

Introduction

Two governments had fallen because of their failure to bring the war with Germany to a satisfactory conclusion; the Bolsheviks were determined not to go the same way. Even Lenin, however, harboured some initial hopes that communist enthusiasm in Russia, or revolution in Germany, might remove the necessity for a humiliating peace treaty. He soon realised that such hopes were unrealistic. Others in his party took some time to reach this conclusion but despite the Left Communists with their hope of revolutionary war and Trotsky with his no war, no peace formula, an ignominious peace was signed at Brest-Litovsk in early 1918.

Lenin proclaimed it as a necessary evil, a breathing space while Russia rebuilt her strength and awaited copycat communist revolutions throughout the rest of Europe but there was no respite at all as the international peace with Germany was the signal for widespread internal disturbances. The civil war, by its very nature, was a confused affair with no definite start or finish. The Bolsheviks – or Communists as they now called themselves – had already made many enemies and the humiliation of Brest-Litovsk provided the final excuse for positive action against the new government. Kornilov escaped imprisonment. Social Revolutionary and Menshevik leaders took over important cities. New governments proclaimed the independence of Finland, the Ukraine, Poland. Ex-tsarist commanders raised White forces. To cap it all, the Allied powers sent in armies of intervention to protect their supplies and force Russia back into the war.

Yet the situation was not as bleak as it first appeared. Kornilov was killed by a stray shell. Tsarist generals found they had little in common with Social Revolutionaries and Mensheviks. There was no one unifying leader, especially after the execution of the tsar by the Bolsheviks. The allies sent few troops and the whole exercise became redundant with the surrender of Germany in November 1918. There were still sufficient British and French troops for the Bolsheviks to be able to play on Russian patriotism and to accuse the Whites of being in the pay of foreigners. In these circumstances most rank and file Mensheviks and Social Revolutionaries fought against the Whites.

The Bolsheviks had a number of advantages: a central defensive area including Petrograd and Moscow, unified command, an efficient army, a single purpose. They also showed some flexibility in their policies. Land was promised to the peasants, a policy few White leaders would agree with. Self-determination for parts of Russia was announced, a policy that the Bolsheviks were too weak to stop anyway. The White forces lacked unity, purpose and popularity. The Bolsheviks were victorious; but the war was ruinous for Russia.

1 Brest–Litovsk

(a) Lenin's initial hopes

Finally, our Party alone can by a victorious insurrection, save Petrograd; for if our proposal for peace is rejected, if we do not secure even an armistice, then we shall become 'defencists', we shall place ourselves at the head of the war parties, we shall be the
5   war party par excellence, and we shall conduct the war in a truly revolutionary manner. We shall take away all the bread and boots from the capitalists. We shall leave them only crusts and dress them in bast shoes. We shall send all the bread and footwear to the front.

And then we shall save Petrograd.
10   The resources, both material and spiritual, for a truly revolutionary war in Russia are still immense; the chances are a hundred to one that the Germans will grant us at least an armistice. And to secure an armistice now would in itself mean to win the whole world.

Lenin, *Marxism and Insurrection*, op cit, p 13

(b) The decree on peace

15   The workers' and peasants' government, created by the Revolution of October 24–25 and basing itself on the Soviets of Workers', Soldiers' and Peasants' Deputies, calls upon all the belligerent peoples and their governments to start immediate negotiations for a just, democratic peace.
20   By a just or democratic peace, for which the overwhelming majority of the working class and other working people of all the belligerent countries, exhausted, tormented and racked by the war, are craving – a peace that has been most definitely and insistently demanded by the Russian workers and peasants ever since the
25   overthrow of the tsarist monarchy – by such a peace the government means an immediate peace without annexations (i.e., without the

seizure of foreign lands, without the forcible incorporation of foreign nations) and without indemnities.

> Report on Peace, 26 October 1917. Reprinted in Lenin, *The October Revolution*, op cit, pp 22–4

(c) The German terms, according to Lenin

The ultimatum is as follows: either the continuation of the war, or
30 a peace with annexations, i.e., peace on condition that we surrender all the territory we have occupied, while the Germans retain all the territory they have occupied and impose upon us an indemnity (outwardly disguised as payment for the maintenance of prisoners) – an indemnity of about three thousand million rubles, payable over
35 a number of years.

The socialist government of Russia is faced with a question – a question whose solution brooks no delay – of whether to accept this peace with annexations now, or to immediately wage a revolutionary war. In fact, no middle course is possible. No further
40 postponement can now be achieved, for we have already done everything possible and impossible to deliberately protract the negotiations.

. . .

Consequently, the situation at present with regard to a revolutionary war is as follows:
45 If the German revolution were to break out and triumph in the coming three or four months, the tactics of an immediate revolutionary war might perhaps not ruin our socialist revolution.

If, however, the German revolution does not occur in the next few months, the course of events, if the war is continued, will
50 inevitably be such that grave defeats will compel Russia to conclude an even more disadvantageous separate peace, a peace, moreover, which would be concluded, not by a socialist government, but by some other (for example, a bloc of the bourgeois Rada and Chernov's followers, or something similar). For the peasant army,
55 which is exhausted to the limit by the war, will after the very first defeats – and very likely within a matter of weeks, and not of months – overthrow the socialist workers' government.

This being the state of affairs, it would be absolutely impermissible tactics to stake the fate of the socialist revolution, which has
60 already begun in Russia, merely on the chance that the German revolution may begin in the immediate future, within a matter of weeks. Such tactics would be a reckless gamble. We have no right to take such risks.

> On the history of the question of the unfortunate peace, 7 January 1918. Reprinted in Lenin, *The Revolutionary Phrase* (Moscow, 1965) pp 8–9

   a According to extract (a), how did Lenin think that the Bolsheviks might still win the war with Germany?

★   *b* Why are the suggestions for peace outlined in extract (b) rather optimistic?

   c How do the German terms in extract (c) differ from those suggested by Lenin in extract (b)?

★   *d* Why did the Bolsheviks pin so much hope on a forthcoming German revolution?

(d) Lenin's reaction

He begins by setting forth the three standpoints brought out at the previous meeting (1) signing a separate annexationist peace, (2) waging a revolutionary war, and (3) proclaiming the war ended, demobilising the army, but not signing a peace treaty. At the
5 previous meeting, the first standpoint received 15 votes, the second 32 and the third 16.
. . .

   Of course, the peace we conclude will be an ignominious one, but we need a breathing space in order to carry out social reforms (take transport alone); we need to consolidate ourselves, and this
10 takes time. We need to complete the crushing of the bourgeoisie, but for this we need to have both our hands free. Once we have done this, we shall free both our hands, and then we should be able to carry on a revolutionary war against international imperialism. The echelons of the revolutionary volunteer army
15 which have now been formed are the officers of our future army.
   What Comrade Trotsky is proposing – an end to the war, refusal to sign a peace treaty and demobilisation of the army – is an international political demonstration.
                 Ibid, pp 18–19

(e) No war, no peace

The Germans lost little time in replying to Trotsky's refusal to sign
20 their peace terms and, to the consternation of the Bolsheviks, began to advance on St. Petersburg. At first the Bolsheviks made some show of resistance. Orders were given in this sense to the fleet and to the army. Trotsky himself, whom I was now seeing daily, informed me that, even if Russia could not resist, she would wage
25 a partisan war to the best of her ability. Very soon, however, it became clear that, in the military sense of the word, there could be no resistance. The Bolsheviks had come into power on a peace slogan. A war slogan might easily bring about their ruin. The bourgeoisie was openly delighted at the prospect of the German

advance, which had emboldened the anti-Bolshevik Press to attack the Bolsheviks with a frenzied fury. The determining factor was the attitude of the troops. On the rumour that the war was to be renewed desertions from the front assumed the proportions of panic flight, and, after an all-night sitting of the Commissars, a telegram was sent to the Germans capitulating entirely and asking for peace on any terms.

. . .

On February 23rd the German terms were received. They were considerably stiffer in their territorial demands than the Treaty of Versailles, and once again the ranks of the Bolsheviks were torn with dissension. The next day, after a fierce and passionate debate, the Central Executive Committee decided by 112 votes to 86 to accept the German terms. Lenin's cold, calculated logic dominated the meeting. There were, however, 25 abstentions. Among them was the vote of Trotsky, who during the discussion remained skulking in his room.

Lockhart, op cit, pp 228–9

(f) Lenin's plans are implemented

Comrade Lenin believes that the policy of revolutionary phrases is at an end. If this policy is continued, he will resign both from the government and from the Central Committee. An army is needed for a revolutionary war, and it does not exist. That means the terms must be accepted.

Comrade Lenin. Some have reproached me for coming out with an ultimatum. I put it as a last resort. It is a mockery for our Central Committee members to talk of an international civil war. There is a civil war in Russia, but not in Germany. Our agitation remains. We are agitating not by words, but by the revolution. That too remains. Stalin is wrong when he says that we need not sign. These terms must be signed. If you don't sign them, you will sign the Soviet power's death warrant within three weeks. These terms do not infringe on the Soviet power. I have not the slightest hesitation. I put the ultimatum in order to withdraw it. I don't want revolutionary phrases. The German revolution has not yet matured. This will take months. The terms must be accepted. If there is another ultimatum later, it will be in a new situation.

Speech at a meeting of the Bolshevik Party, 23 February 1918. Reprinted in Lenin, *The Revolutionary Phrase*, op cit, p 38

(g) Bolshevik opponents of the peace

These conditions cut off the centres of revolution from the producing regions which feed industry, divide the centres of the

workers' movement, destroying a number of its largest centres (Latvia, Ukraine), undermine the economic policy of socialism (question of the annulment of loans, the socialization of production, etc.), bring to nothing the international significance of the Russian
70 Revolution (renunciation of international propaganda), turn the Soviet Republic into a tool of imperialist policy (Persia, Afghanistan), last of all, attempt to disarm it (demand that old and new units be demobilized). All this does not give the possibility of a breathing-space, but places the struggle of the proletariat in worse
75 conditions than ever.

Without giving any real postponement, the signing of the peace saps the revolutionary will of the proletariat to struggle and holds back the development of the international revolution. Therefore the sole correct tactics could be the tactics of revolutionary war
80 against imperialism.

In view of the complete disintegration of the old army, the remnants of which are worse than useless, revolutionary war in its first stage can only be a war of flying partisan detachments, which will pull into the struggle both the city proletariat and the poorest
85 peasantry and will transform military activities on our side into a civil war of the working classes against international capital. Such a war, whatever defeats it might bring in the beginning, would inevitably disintegrate the forces of imperialism.

Theses on War and Peace by opponents of peace, 6–8 March 1918. Printed in Chamberlain, vol I, op cit, pp 501–2

(h) Lenin's reply to criticism

It is a fact that at a moment when the army at the front, being in
90 no condition to fight, is fleeing in panic, abandoning its guns and not even stopping to blow up bridges, the defence of the fatherland and the raising of its defence capacity lie not in babbling about a revolutionary war (to babble in the face of this panic-stricken flight of the army – not one detachment of which was stopped by the
95 advocates of revolutionary war – is downright shameful), but in retreating in good order, so as to save the remnants of the army, taking advantage of every day's respite for this purpose.

Facts are stubborn things.
. . .

N. Bukharin is now even attempting to deny the fact that he
100 and his friends asserted that it was impossible for the Germans to attack. But very, very many people know that it is a fact, that Bukharin and his friends did assert this, and that by sowing such an illusion they helped German imperialism and hindered the growth of the German revolution, which has now been weakened
105 by the fact that the Great-Russian Soviet Republic, during the panic-stricken flight of the peasant army, has been deprived of

thousands upon thousands of guns and of wealth to the value of
hundreds upon hundreds of millions.
. . .
And if the new terms are worse, more onerous and humiliating
110 than the bad, onerous and humiliating Brest terms, it is our pseudo-
Lefts, Bukharin, Lomov, Uritsky and Co., who are to blame for
this happening to the Great-Russian Soviet Republic. This is a
historical fact, as is proved by the voting referred to above. It is a
fact you cannot escape, wriggle as you will. You were offered the
115 Brest terms, and you replied by blustering and swaggering, which
led to worse terms. That is a fact. And you cannot absolve
yourselves of the responsibility for it.
   A Serious Lesson and a Serious Responsibility. Reprinted in
   Lenin, *The Revolutionary Phrase*, op cit, pp 67–70

Questions

★   a   Explain the following references in extract (d):
          (i) 'a separate annexationist peace' (line 2);
          (ii) 'a revolutionary war' (line 3).
★   b   What does Lenin mean by his description of Trotsky's policy
          as 'an international political demonstration' (line 18)?
    c   How successful was Trotsky's policy, according to extract (e)?
          What impression of him is given in this extract?
    d   According to Lenin's arguments in extract (f), why must the
          Bolsheviks sign the peace treaty with Germany?
    e   Assess the arguments for and against the signing of the treaty
          in extracts (g) and (h).

2   Civil War Factions

(a) *Kornilov's political programme*

The general principles of Kornilov's political program are as
follows:
(1) To re-establish the rights of citizens: All Russian citizens
without distinction of sex or nationality shall be equal before the
5   law. All class privileges are to be abolished and the inviolability of
home and person, freedom of travel, and of choosing one's residence
will be safeguarded, etc.
(2) To re-establish full freedom of speech and of the press.
(3) To re-establish freedom of industry and commerce and to
10 abolish nationalization of private financial enterprises.
(4) To re-establish private property.
(5) To re-establish the Russian Army on the basis of strict military
discipline. The army should be formed on a volunteer basis (after
the British model) without committees, commissars, or elective
15 officers.

(6) Russia must assume all obligations arising from the treaties with the Allies. The war must be brought to an end in close co-operation with the Allies; peace must be general, honorable, and on democratic principles, i.e., with the right of self-determination
20 for oppressed nations.

. . .

(8) The Constituent Assembly dissolved by the Bolsheviks should be restored. . . .

. . .

(11) The solution of the complicated land question will be left to the Constituent Assembly. Pending that solution . . . no anarchical
25 seizures (of land) by individual citizens will be tolerated.

Quoted in Bunyan and Fisher, op cit, pp 424–5

(b) Kolchak on the land question

The gallant armies of the Russian Government are moving forward into the territory of European Russia. They are approaching those basic Russian provinces where land is an object of disputes, where no one is convinced of his right to the land and of the possibility
30 of reaping the fruits of his labour.

Our motherland, which was once rich in bread, is now poor and hungry. It is the duty of the Government to create in the agricultural population a sense of calm and firm assurance that the harvest will belong to those who now till the land, who have ploughed and
35 sowed it.

The Government therefore states that everyone who now posses-ses the land; everyone who sowed it and worked on it, whether he was the owner or the renter, has the right to gather in the harvest. Moreover, the Government will take measures to provide in the
40 future for the landless peasants and for those who have little land, utilizing, first of all, the land of private owners and of the state which has already passed into the actual possession of the peasantry.

Those lands which were formerly tilled entirely or predominantly by the resources of the families of the owners of the land, individual
45 holders and those who separated from the village community, are to be restored to their legal owners.

The measures which have been adopted aim to satisfy the urgent needs of the working population of the villages. The ancient land problem will be finally decided by the National Assembly.
50 Legislative acts about the regulation of land relations, about the method of temporarily utilizing land which has been seized, about the subsequent just distribution of such lands, finally, about the conditions of compensating former owners will follow in the near future.
55 The general objectives of these laws will be: the transfer of the use of land from non-workers to workers, and widespread co-

operation in the development of small working households, irrespective of whether these will be based on personal or on community ownership of the land. In order to promote the passing of the land into the possession of working peasant households, the Government will open up wide opportunities for acquiring full property rights in these lands.

Chamberlain, vol I, op cit, pp 481–2

(c) White Army behaviour

... U.S.A. Commander-in-Chief in Siberia, General W. S. Graves writes:

'At no time while I was in Siberia was there enough popular support behind Koltchak in Eastern Siberia for him or the people supporting him to have lasted one month if all Allied supports had been removed.' ...

Koltchak was suspected, not without reason, of Tsarist leanings. Certainly he was entirely devoid of any bias in favour of democracy. He hated and in return was hated by the Social Revolutionaries, who at that time were far and away the largest political body in Siberia. From the first his regime was distrusted and detested by all but the military clique who created it.

The French looked upon it with deep suspicion, scenting British intrigue. ...

The Czechs – the backbone of the armed forces in Siberia – were profoundly hostile, and on November 20 the Czech National Council published a manifesto expressing their hostility. 'The coup d'état' – so ran the document – 'goes against those elementary laws which should be the foundation of all governments. We who are fighting for the ideal of liberty ... will not give our help or sympathy to coups d'état which are in opposition to those principles.'

But deepest and most ominous of all was the hostility of the common people, who received this new dictatorship with a mistrust and alarm that grew in intensity. ...

All the old vices of the Tsarist regime came back. ... Floggings and shootings once more became the basis of army organization. The officers gambled, drank, and stole military supplies, whilst the men starved.

The anti-democratic colour of the new government became clearer every day. Representatives of workmen were no longer admitted to official receptions, and the agrarian policy of the government plainly showed that the clock had been set back to pre-revolutionary times.

Meanwhile a White Terror was inaugurated, far worse than anything perpetrated by the Reds. ... Not merely suspected Bolsheviks, but Socialists of any kind, even Liberals and Democrats,

100 were slaughtered in thousands. . . . In one village on the Amur a
    number of intelligentsia – Democrats – had taken refuge. . . .
    Koltchak's governor . . . encircled the place with White troops; a
    hole was made in the ice on the river and the entire population
    driven under the ice.

    Quoted in S. W. Page, *Russia in Revolution* (New Jersey,
    1965) pp 152–3

(d) White Army problems

105 But Denikin's dangers grew with his conquests. He became
    responsible for a large part of Russia without any of the resources –
    moral, political, or material – needed to restore prosperity and
    contentment. The population, which welcomed his troops and
    dreaded the Bolsheviks, were too cowed by the terrible years
110 through which they had passed to make any vigorous rally in his
    support. The responsibility for the administrative well-being of
    great cities and provinces in a time of dearth and confusion, with
    crumbling railways and arrested commerce, fell upon a blunt,
    stouthearted military man with a newly acquired taste for political
115 affairs, who has already overburdened with the organization of his
    army and the conduct of the war. The political elements which had
    gathered around him were weak, mixed and fiercely divided upon
    essentials. Some urged him to display the Imperial standards and
    advance in the name of the Czar. This alone would confront
120 Bolshevism with insignia equally well understood on either side
    by all. The majority of his advisers and principal officers made it
    clear that they would not tolerate such a decision. Others urged
    him to proclaim that the land should be left to the peasants who
    had seized it. To whom it was replied: 'Are we then no better than
125 the Bolsheviks?' But the worst cleavage arose upon the policy
    towards the countries or provinces which had broken away from
    Russia. Denikin stood for the integrity of the Russian Fatherland
    as he understood it. He was therefore the foe of his own allies in
    the war against the Soviets. The Baltic States, struggling for life
130 against Bolshevik force and propaganda, could make no common
    cause with the Russian General who denied their right to indepen-
    dence. The Poles, who provided the largest and strongest army at
    war with the Soviets, saw that they would have to defend themselves
    against Denikin on the morrow of a joint victory. The Ukraine
135 was ready to fight the Bolsheviks for independence, but were not
    attracted by the military government of Denikin.

    Winston S. Churchill, *The Aftermath* (1941) pp 252–3

★ *a* In what ways is extract (a) an attack on the Bolsheviks?
   b Compare the attitude adopted towards the land question in extracts (a) and (b).
★ *c* Who might support the policies outlined in these two extracts?
   d What criticisms are made of Kolchak's army in extract (c)?
   e What problems did Denikin face, according to extract (d)?
   f How does this extract try to absolve Denikin from most personal blame for his desperate situation?

(e) Declaration of the Rights of the Peoples of Russia

. . . The first Congress of Soviets, in June of this year, proclaimed the rights of the peoples of Russia to self-determination. The second Congress of Soviets, in November last, confirmed this inalienable right of the peoples of Russia more decisively and definitely.

5   Executing the will of these Congresses, the Council of People's Commissars has resolved to establish as a basis for its activity in the question of Nationalities, the following principles:
(1) The equality and sovereignty of the peoples of Russia.
(2) The right of the peoples of Russia to free self-determination,
10 even to the point of separation and the formation of an independent state.
. . .
The Central Rada at Kiev immediately declared Ukraine an independent republic, as did the Government of Finland, through the Senate at Helsingfors. Independent 'Governments' sprang up
15 in Siberia and the Caucasus. The Polish troops in the Russian Army, abolished their committees and established an iron discipline. . . .
All these 'Governments' and 'movements' had two characteristics in common; they were controlled by the propertied classes and they feared and detested Bolshevism. . . .
        Reed, op cit, p 231

(f) A Bolshevik Decree to the Ukrainian Rada

20 We accuse the Rada of playing, under the guise of nationalism, a double game, a game which for some time expressed itself in the Rada's refusal to recognize the Soviets and the Soviet power in the Ukraine (among other things, the Rada refused to call . . . a regional congress of Soviets). This double game, which is the chief
25 reason why we cannot recognize the Rada as the plenipotentiary representative of the toiling and exploited masses of the Ukrainian Republic, has of late led the Rada to undertake a number of steps which preclude the possibility of any agreement.
In the first place, the Rada is disorganizing the front . . . by

30   moving about and recalling the Ukrainian units. . . .

In the second place, the Rada is disarming the Soviet troops stationed in the Ukraine.

In the third place, the Rada is supporting the Cadet–Kaledin plot. . . .

Quoted in Bunyan and Fisher, op cit, p 220

(g) The Rada's reply

35   The declaration of the Sovnarkom, in which the independence of the Ukrainian People's Republic is recognized, lacks either sincerity or logic. It is not possible simultaneously to recognize the right of a people to self-determination including separation and at the same time to infringe roughly on that right by imposing on the
40   people in question a certain type of government. . . . The General Secretariat categorically repudiates all attempts on the part of the People's Commissars to interfere in the political life of the Ukrainian People's Republic. The pretensions of the People's Commissars to guide the Ukrainian democracy are the less justifiable since the
45   political organization which they wish to impose on the Ukraine has led to unenviable results in the territory which is under their own control. Great Russia is more and more becoming the prey of anarchy and economic and political disruption, while the most arbitrary rule and the abuse of all liberties gained by the revolution
50   . . . reign supreme in your land. The General Secretariat does not wish to repeat that sad experiment in the Ukraine.

Ibid, op cit, p 221

(h) Bolshevik support in Russia

The Constituent Assembly elections in Russia in November 1917, compared with the two-year civil war of 1917–19, are highly instructive in this respect.

55   See which districts proved to be the least Bolshevik. First, the East-Urals and the Siberian where the Bolsheviks polled 12 per cent and 10 per cent of the votes respectively. Secondly, the Ukraine where the Bolsheviks polled 10 per cent of the votes. Of the other districts, the Bolsheviks polled the smallest percentage of votes in
60   the peasant district of Great Russia, the Volga-Black Earth district, but even there the Bolsheviks polled 16 per cent of the votes.

It was precisely in the districts where the Bolsheviks polled the lowest percentage of votes in November 1917 that the counter-revolutionary forces had the greatest success. It was precisely in
65   those districts that the rule of Kolchak and Denikin lasted for months and months.

The vacillation of the petty-bourgeois population was particularly marked in those districts where the influence of the proletariat is

weakest. Vacillation was at first in favour of the Bolsheviks when
70 they granted land and when the demobilised soldiers brought the
news about peace; later – against the Bolsheviks when, to promote
the international development of the revolution and to protect its
centre in Russia, they agreed to sign the Treaty of Brest and thereby
'offended' patriotic sentiments, the deepest of petty-bourgeois
75 sentiments. The dictatorship of the proletariat was particularly
displeasing to the peasants in those places where there were the
largest stocks of surplus grain, when the Bolsheviks showed that
they would strictly and firmly secure the transfer of those surplus
stocks to the state at fixed prices. The peasants in the Urals, Siberia
80 and the Ukraine turned to Kolchak and Denikin.

Further, the experience of Kolchak and Denikin 'democracy',
about which every hack writer in Kolchakia and Denikia shouted
in every issue of the whiteguard newspapers, showed the peasants
that phrases about democracy and about the 'Constituent Assembly'
85 serve only as a screen to conceal the dictatorship of the landowners
and capitalists.

Another turn towards Bolshevism began and peasant revolts in
the rear of Kolchak and Denikin. The peasants welcomed the Red
troops as liberators.

> The Constituent Assembly Elections. Reprinted in Lenin,
> *October Revolution*, op cit, p 270

Questions

  a Describe the policy of self-determination outlined in extract (e).
★ *b* Why does the author of extract (e) write 'Governments' and
'movements' rather than governments and movements (line
17)?
  c Analyse the arguments for and against the Rada in extracts (f)
and (g).
★ *d* Why did the Bolsheviks initially support the policy of self-
determination?
  e According to extract (h), which parts of Russia provided the
least support for the Bolsheviks?
★ *f* Analyse the Bolsheviks' arguments on why their support was
strong at some times and weak at others as outlined in this
extract.

3 Foreign Intervention

(a) *Allied proposals*

The Allied and Associated Powers feel that the time has come when
it is necessary for them once more to make clear the policy they
propose to pursue in regard to Russia.

It has always been a cardinal axiom of the Allied and Associated Powers to avoid interference in the internal affairs of Russia. Their original intervention was made for the sole purpose of assisting those elements in Russia which wanted to continue the struggle against German autocracy and to free their country from German rule, and in order to rescue the Czechoslovaks from the danger of annihilation at the hands of the Bolshevist forces.

The Allied and Associated Governments now wish to declare formally that the object of their policy is to restore peace within Russia by enabling the Russian people to resume control of their own affairs through the instrumentality of a freely elected constituent assembly, and to restore peace along its frontiers by arranging for the settlement of disputes in regard to the boundaries of the Russian State and its relations with its neighbours through the peaceful arbitration of the League of Nations.

They are convinced by their experience of the last twelve months that it is not possible to attain these ends by dealing with the Soviet Government of Moscow. They are therefore disposed to assist the government of Admiral Koltchak and his associates with munitions, supplies, and food to establish themselves as the government of all Russia, provided they receive from them definite guarantees that their policy has the same object in view as the Allied and Associated Powers.

With this object they would ask Admiral Koltchak and his associates whether they would agree to the following as the conditions under which they would accept continued assistance from the Allied and Associated Powers.

In the first place as soon as they reach Moscow that they will summon a constituent assembly elected by a free, secret, and democratic franchise, as the supreme legislature for Russia, to which the government of Russia must be responsible, or, if at that time order is not sufficiently restored, they will summon the Constituent Assembly, elected in 1917, to sit until such time as new elections are possible.

Secondly – that throughout the areas which they at present control they will permit free elections in the normal course for all free and legally constituted assemblies, such as municipalities, Zemstvos, etc.

Thirdly – that they will countenance no attempt to revive the special privilege of any class or order in Russia. The Allied and Associated Powers have noted with satisfaction the solemn declaration made by Admiral Koltchak and his associates, that they have no intention of restoring the former land system.

Fourthly – that the independence of Finland and Poland be recognized, and that in the event of the frontiers and other relations between Russia and these countries not being settled by agreement, they will be referred to the arbitration of the League of Nations.

Churchill, op cit, pp 180–1

(b) British worries in Romania

I quite understand that our first object is to assist to establish some power or force in South of Russia as for instance Ukraine Rada,
55 on which Roumanian Army can then retire. This however, raises the big question whether such assistance should be open or secret.

Open assistance would give great moral encouragement to all parties who are opposed to Bolsheviks: Rada though it has declared for peace would make at least some show of sympathy if openly
60 recognized: Cossacks might come in: many thousands of Russian officers would join movement: it might secure us Black Sea Fleet: it might upset Bolsheviks.

But disadvantages are that it recognises the break up of Russia: it would mean open opposition to Bolsheviks: it would give them
65 excuse they may be looking for to [?revoke] Alliance: they would then openly oppose us and give over to Germans their guns and German prisoners. Another disadvantage is that Bolsheviks might defeat Rada in which case we should have done no good.

Secret assistance can be given chiefly in money: it can be disbursed
70 in buying supplies and also in various secret societies with whom we can get into touch, and does not commit us in any way. But we have no guarantee as to how far it will be used in the right direction and is therefore a pure gamble.

Another disadvantage is that Rada will not be content with
75 anything short of official recognition.

The second object is to prolong armistice and negotiations in the hope that Bolsheviks may be upset in the meanwhile.

At the end of the armistice there is no force in Southern Russia on which Roumanians can fall back, we must then acquiesce in
80 Roumanian Government making peace.

Our third object in this case will be to see that interests of Allies are as far as possible safeguarded: these interests are that Roumanian arms and locomotives should not be handed over to Germans. It is quite certain that Roumanians will not consent to destroy either
85 arms or locomotives, but, we can [?intimate] to them that if they are given over to Germans we shall repudiate all other obligations to Roumania.

Public Record Office: The British Ambassador in Romania, 22 December 1917. FO 371 3019

(c) A British critic

Obviously, the British Government was faced with a problem of immense difficulty. It was not in a position to send large forces to
90 Russia. If it supported the small officer armies in the South, it ran the risk of driving the Bolsheviks into an unholy league with the Germans. If it supported the Bolsheviks, there was, at the beginning

at any rate, a serious danger that the Germans would advance on Moscow and St. Petersburg and set up their own pro-German
95 bourgeois Government. . . .

Moreover, it was physically impossible for our Government to keep pace with the situation, which changed radically every forty-eight hours. That British Ministers were unable to see any sign of order in the prevailing chaos was natural enough. Where they were
100 to blame was in listening to too many counsellors and in not realising the fundamental truth that in Russia the educated class represented only an infinitesimal minority, without organisation or political experience and without any contact with the masses. . . .

London, however, continued to regard it as a passing storm,
105 after which the glass would return to 'set fair'. The most dangerous of all historical aphorisms is the catch-phrase: 'plus ca change, plus c'est la même chose'. During the spring and summer of 1918 it was constantly on the lips of the British pro–interventionists.

Lockhart, op cit, p 264

(d) Allied landings

On August 4th Moscow went wild with excitement. The Allies
110 had landed at Archangel. For several days the city was a prey to rumour. The Allies had landed in strong force. Some stories put the figure at 100,000. No estimate was lower than two divisions. The Japanese were to send seven divisions through Siberia to help the Czechs. Even the Bolsheviks lost their heads and, in despair,
115 began to pack their archives. In the middle of this crisis I saw Karachan. He spoke of the Bolsheviks as lost. They would, however, never surrender. They would go underground and continue the struggle to the last. . . .

For forty-eight hours I deluded myself with the thought that the
120 intervention might prove a brilliant success. . . .

But that afternooon, when I saw Karachan, I had misgivings. His face was wreathed in smiles. The dejection of the previous days had gone, and his relief was too obvious to be put down to play-acting. 'The situation is not serious,' he said. 'The Allies have
125 landed only a few hundred men.' . . .

We had committed the unbelievable folly of landing at Archangel with fewer than twelve hundred men.

In the absence of a strong lead from the Allies the various counter-revolutionary groups began to quarrel and bicker among
130 themselves. The accuracy of my dictum that the support we would receive from the Russians would be in direct proportion to the number of troops we sent ourselves was speedily proved. The broad masses of the Russian people remained completely apathetic.

Ibid, pp 308–10

(e) Lenin's response

We have been defencists since October 25, 1917; we have won the
135 right to defend our native land. It is not secret treaties that we are
defending, we have annulled and exposed them to the whole world.
We are defending our country against the imperialists. We are
defending and we shall win. It is not the Great Power status of
Russia that we are defending – of that nothing is left but Russia
140 proper – nor is it national interests, for we assert that the interests
of socialism, of world socialism are higher than national interests,
higher than the interests of the state. We are defenders of the
socialist fatherland.

> Report on Foreign Policy, 14 May 1918. Reprinted in Lenin,
> *The October Revolution*, op cit, p 121

Questions

a According to extract (a), how had the reasons for Allied intervention in Russia changed and why?

b Compare the Allies' conditions for Admiral Kolchak outlined in this extract with those put forward by Kornilov and Kolchak on pages 93–5.

c What arguments for and against intervention by the British are put forward in extract (b)?

d What criticisms of the British government are made by the author of extract (c)?

e In what ways was British intervention a mistake, according to extract (d)?

f In extract (e), what is a defencist (line 134)?

g What appeal does Lenin make in extract (e)?

★ h Why did the Bolsheviks win the civil war?

VII Domestic Policy

Introduction

After the October Revolution it soon became clear that the Bolsheviks had no intention of sharing their victory with anyone else. This should not have appeared that surprising: Marxist leaders had always taken for granted that communism was totally correct and that all other parties were wrong. There was no room for the western, democratic idea that no party had a monopoly of the truth. Once in power the dictatorship of the proletariat must be strong to force people to be free, for them to accept the ideas of equality and sharing. At the same time this theory made it easy to destroy any alternate power base such as the trade unions without setting any date for the government to dissolve itself and let the state wither away.

Marxist principles might be fixed but policies were not and Lenin in particular was very adept at being flexible in the face of certain realities. Workers' control was essential, eventually, but in the short term the temporary drop in output this would cause was unacceptable in the middle of a civil war; so the Bolsheviks kept on some of the old managers. In agriculture, the Bolsheviks believed in state ownership of the land but the peasants had already taken hold of it. This Lenin also accepted, if holding on to the idea of eventual state control. The Bolsheviks had always been weak in the country and moves to order the peasants were far from successful. War Communism, the attempt to seize food from recalcitrant peasants who still found no incentive to swap surplus food for worthless money, met with limited success.

Other aspects of stricter Bolshevik control worked better: the reintroduction of secret police; a systematic Red Terror; the censorship of the press. All these measures were seen as necessary in wartime. Most were to continue in peacetime as well. It was soon realised that the Provisional government had been a brief interlude in traditional Russian politics. There was little difference between the secret police of the tsar and those of the Bolsheviks; except the latter were, perhaps, more efficient.

1 Party Politics

(a) The Bolshevik government

The negotiations, which seemed promising, soon began to drag.
On the one hand, the Bolsheviks became less accommodating as
they saw their power consolidating, on the other the remaining
Socialist parties showed less and less inclination to work with
5 people who obviously relied on force and expulsion to achieve
their object. The town Duma, which protested from the first
against the rising, took an active part in the negotiations, but M.
Schreider, the Mayor, declared, as the spokesman of the only
legally elected body in Petrograd, that the municipal delegates
10 would have instructions to demand the immediate release of all the
Ministers and other arrested persons, to maintain the legal existence
of the late Government until a new one was regularly formed to
oppose any Bolshevik participation in the Cabinet, and to work
for the creation of a new body, mainly drawn from the various
15 municipalities to which the Government would be responsible.

For a time attention was fixed on this last point. The railwaymen
proposed that the assembly should consist of 120 persons, 100 of
whom would represent the municipalities of Petrograd and Moscow
and most of the rest be drawn from the Soviets. The Bolsheviks
20 proposed that the Government should be responsible to the new
executive committee of the all-Russian Soviet to which should be
added Representatives of the peasants, the army, the fleet, the trades
unions and the socialists in the municipalities. . . .

As regards the composition of the Government, the Bolsheviks
25 declared definitely on November 17th that half the Ministries at
least must be held by them and that they would occupy those of
Foreign Affairs, the Interior and Labour. On the following day
some ten Commissaries of the people resigned, Kamanev and
Zinoviev amongst them, owing to the refusal of M. M. Lenin and
30 Trotsky to allow liberty of the Press or to meet the views of the
other Socialist parties. The Duma, the railwaymen and the peasants'
delegates also dropped their negotiations, and the unregenerate
minority, backed by the sailors and the Red Guard, are left in
undisputed possession of the field, in defiance of the solemn decree
35 of the Senate that the late Government remains in existence until
the Constituent Assembly shall have elected another.

> Public Record Office, Summary of Recent Events,
> FO 371 300

(b) The abolition of political parties

On June 14, 1918, the All-Russia Central Executive Committee
passed the following decree. 'Taking into consideration (1) that
Soviet power is going through a very difficult period when it has

40 to repulse the onslaught of international imperialism on all the
fronts simultaneously and also its allies within the Russian Republic
who resort to any means in their struggle against the Workers' and
Peasants' Government starting with bare-faced calumny and ending
with a conspiracy and an armed revolt; (2) that it is absolutely
45 intolerable to have in the Soviet bodies representatives of the parties
which are obviously trying to discredit the power of the Soviets
and to overthrow it; (3) that it has transpired from the earlier
published documents as well as from the documents read out at
the present meeting that representatives of the parties of Socialist-
50 Revolutionaries (Right and Centrists) and of the R.S.D.L.P. (Mensheviks) were exposed as organisers of armed revolts against the
workers and peasants in collusion with the open counter-
revolutionaries – Kaledin and Kornilov on the Don, Dutov in the
Urals, Semyonov, Khorvat and Kolchak in Siberia, and recently
55 together with the Czechoslovaks and the Black-Hundred bands
who had joined the latter.

'The All-Russia Central Executive Committee resolves to expel
from the All-Russia C.E.C. the representatives of the parties of the
S.R.s (Right and Centrists) and of the R.S.D.L.P. (Mensheviks),
60 and also proposes to all Soviets of Workers', Soldiers', Peasants'
and Cossacks' Deputies to expel the representatives of these groups
from their midst.'

Lenin, *The October Revolution*, op cit, p 392

(c) The dictatorship of the proletariat

Either the dictatorship of Kornilov (if we take him as the Russian
type of bourgeois Cavaignac), or the dictatorship of the proletariat –
65 any other choice is out of the question for a country which is
developing at an extremely rapid rate with extremely sharp turns
and amidst desperate ruin created by one of the most horrible wars
in history. Every solution that offers a middle path is either a
deception of the people by the bourgeoisie – for the bourgeoisie
70 dare not tell the truth, dare not say that they need Kornilov –
or an expression of the dull-wittedness of the petty-bourgeois
democrats, of the Chernovs, Tseretelis and Martovs, who chatter
about the unity of democracy, the dictatorship of democracy, the
general democratic front, and similar nonsense. Those whom even
75 the progress of the Russian revolution of 1917–18 has not taught
that a middle course is impossible, must be given up for lost. . . .

On the other hand, it is not difficult to see that during every
transition from capitalism to socialism, dictatorship is necessary for
two main reasons, or along two main channels. Firstly, capitalism
80 cannot be defeated and eradicated without the ruthless suppression
of the resistance of the exploiters who cannot at once be deprived
of their wealth, of their advantages of organisation and knowledge,

and consequently for a fairly long period will inevitably try to overthrow the hated rule of the poor; secondly, every great
85 revolution, and a socialist revolution in particular, even if there is no external war, is inconceivable without internal war, i.e., civil war, which is even more devastating than external war, and involves thousands and millions of cases of wavering and desertion from one side to another, implies a state of extreme indefiniteness,
90 lack of equilibrium and chaos.

> Lenin, *The Immediate Tasks of the Soviet Government*, op cit, pp 28–30

Questions

a   In extract (a), what problems were there in forming the first government after the fall of the Provisional Government?

b   According to this extract, why did Kamanev and Zinoviev resign from the Bolshevik government?

★   c   Why did Lenin and the Bolsheviks disagree with the idea of a coalition government?

d   According to extract (b), why did the Bolsheviks expel the representatives of other political parties?

e   In extract (c), why is the dictatorship of the proletariat necessary?

(d) Early Bolshevik achievements

We speak of 'the first steps' of communism in Russia (it is also put that way in our Party Programme adopted in March 1919), because all these things have been only partially effected in our country, or, to put it differently, their achievement is only in its early stages.
5 We accomplished instantly, at one revolutionary blow, all that can, in general, be accomplished instantly; on the first day of the dictatorship of the proletariat, for instance, on October 26 (November 8), 1917, the private ownership of land was abolished without compensation for the big landowners – the big landowners
10 were expropriated. Within the space of a few months practically all the big capitalists, owners of factories, joint-stock companies, banks, railways, and so forth, were also expropriated without compensation. The state organisation of large-scale production in industry and the transition from 'workers' control' to 'workers'
15 management' of factories and railways – this had, by and large, already been accomplished; but in relation to agriculture it has only just begun ('state farms', i.e., large farms organised by the workers' state on state-owned land).

> Economics and Politics in the Era of the Dictatorship of the Proletariat (30 October 1919) Quoted in Lenin, *The October Revolution*, op cit, p 235

(e) The first year of Bolshevik rule

And so, comrades, when we ask ourselves what big changes we
20 have made over the past year, we can say the following: from
workers' control, the working class' first steps, and from disposing
of all the country's resources, we are now on the threshold of
creating a workers' administration of industry; from the general
peasants' struggle for land, the peasants struggle against the
25 landowners, a struggle that had a national, bourgeois–democratic
character, we have now reached a stage where the proletarian and
semi–proletarian elements in the countryside have set themselves
apart: those who labour and are exploited have set themselves apart
from the others and have begun to build a new life; the most
30 oppressed country folk are fighting the bourgeoisie, including their
own rural kulak bourgeoisie, to the bitter end.

Furthermore, from the first steps of Soviet organisation we have
now reached a stage where, as Comrade Sverdlov justly remarked
in opening this congress, there is no place in Russia, however
35 remote, where Soviet authority has not asserted itself and become
an integral part of the Soviet Constitution, which is based on long
experience gained in the struggle of the working and oppressed
people. I want to say a few words about the road we have covered,
about this transitional stage.
40 At first our slogan was workers' control. We said that despite
all the promises of the Kerensky government, the capitalists were
continuing to sabotage production and increase dislocation. We can
now see that this would have ended in complete collapse. So the
first fundamental step that every socialist, workers' government
45 has to take is workers' control. We did not decree socialism
immediately throughout industry, because socialism can only take
shape and be consolidated when the working class has learnt how
to run the economy and when the authority of the working people
has been firmly established. Socialism is mere wishful thinking
50 without that. That is why we introduced workers' control, appreciat-
ing that it was a contradictory and incomplete measure, but an
essential one so that the workers themselves might tackle the
momentous tasks of building up industry in a vast country without
and opposed to exploiters.
55 Everyone who took a direct, or even indirect, part in this work,
everyone who lived through all the oppression and brutality of the
old capitalist regime, learned a great deal. We know that little has
been accomplished. We know that in this extremely backward and
impoverished country where innumerable obstacles and barriers
60 were put in the workers' way, it will take them a long time to
learn to run industry. But we consider it most important and
valuable that the workers have themselves tackled the job, and that
we have passed from workers' control, which in all the main
branches of industry was bound to be chaotic, disorganised,

65   primitive and incomplete, to workers' industrial administration on
a national scale.

    The trade unions' position has altered. Their main function now
is to send their representatives to all management boards and central
bodies, to all the new organisations which have taken over a ruined
70   and deliberately sabotaged industry from capitalism. They have
coped with industry without the assistance of those intellectuals
who from the very outset deliberately used their knowledge and
education – the result of mankind's store of knowledge – to frustrate
the cause of socialism, rather than assist the people in building up
75   a socially-owned economy without exploiters. These men wanted
to use their knowledge to put a spoke in the wheel, to hamper
the workers who were least trained for tackling the job of
administration.

    We may have had great difficulties in industry, where we had to
80   cover a road which to many seemed long, but which was actually
short and led from workers' control to workers' administration,
yet far greater preparatory work had to be done in the more
backward countryside.

    6th Congress of Soviets (6 November 1918). Ibid, p 131–3

Questions

a   What were the first achievements of the Bolshevik government
according to extract (d)?

b   In extract (e), what was workers' control? Why did socialism
in industry not take place immediately?

c   What was the new role of the trade unions according to this
extract?

★   d   Why had less been achieved by the Bolsheviks in the country?

2   The Peasants and Agriculture

(a) *A Bolshevik Resolution on agrarian policy*

The Conference considers that land reform can be carried out only
by the Constituent Assembly and that at the present time – pending
the carrying out of such a reform – only temporary adjustments in
land tenure arrangements are possible through the offices of local
5   democratic institutions (land committees, food committees).

    The Conference calls on all party workers to implant this idea in
the consciousness of the peasant masses by means of verbal and
written agitation and to combat energetically any anarchistic seizures
of land or other arbitrary solutions of the question, explaining to
10   the peasant masses that resolving the agrarian question by such
methods can only lead to internecine strife within the ranks of the

peasantry itself as well as paving the way for counter-revolution.
Quoted in Elwood, vol 2, op cit, p 135

(b) The Bolshevik mandate on land

The land question in its full scope can be settled only by the popular
Constituent Assembly.
15   The most equitable settlement of the land question is to be as
follows:
(1) Private ownership of land shall be abolished for ever; land shall
not be sold, purchased, leased, mortgaged, or otherwise alienated.
All land, whether state, crown, monastery, church, factory,
20 entailed, private, public, peasant, etc., shall be confiscated without
compensation and become the property of the whole people, and
pass into the use of all those who cultivate it.
Persons who suffer by this property revolution shall be deemed
to be entitled to public support only for the period necessary for
25 adaption to the new conditions of life.
(2) All mineral wealth – ore, oil, coal, salt, etc., and also all forests
and waters of state importance, shall pass into the exclusive use of
the state. All the small streams, lakes, woods, etc., shall pass into
the use of the communes, to be administered by the local self-
30 government bodies.
(3) Lands on which high-level scientific farming is practised –
orchards, plantations, seed plots, nurseries, hot houses, etc., – shall
not be divided up, but shall be converted into model farms, to be
turned over for exclusive use to the state or to the communes,
35 depending on the size and importance of such lands.
Second All Russian Congress of Soviets (25 October 1917).
Quoted in Lenin, *On the Alliance of the Working Class and
Peasantry* (Moscow, 1970) pp 113–14

(c) Lenin on attracting peasant support

The proletariat can, and must, at once, or at all events very quickly,
win from the bourgeoisie and from petty-bourgeois democrats
'their' masses, i.e., the masses which follow them – win them by
satisfying their most urgent economic needs in a revolutionary way
40 by expropriating the landowners and the bourgeoise. . . .
That is exactly how the Russian proletariat won the peasantry
from the Socialist-Revolutionaries and won them literally a few
hours after achieving state power; a few hours after the victory
over the bourgeoisie in Petrograd, the victorious proletariat issued
45 a 'decree on land', and in that decree it entirely, at once, with
revolutionary swiftness, energy and devotion, satisfied all the
most urgent economic needs of the majority of the peasants, it
expropriated the landowners, entirely and without compensation.

To prove to the peasants that the proletarians did not want to
50   steam-roller them, did not want to boss them, but to help them
and be their friends, the victorious Bolsheviks did not put a single
word of their own into that 'decree on land', but copied it, word
for word, from the peasant mandates (the most revolutionary of
them, of course) which the Socialist-Revolutionaries had published
55   in the Socialist-Revolutionary newspaper.
The Socialist-Revolutionaries fumed and raved, protested and
howled that 'the Bolsheviks had stolen their programme', but they
were only laughed at for that; a fine party, indeed, which had to be
defeated and driven from the government in order that everything in
60   its programme that was revolutionary and of benefit to the working
people could be carried out!

> The Constituent Assembly Elections. Quoted in Lenin, *The
> October Revolution*, op cit, pp 267–8

(d) The response of a social revolutionary

We got into conversation with a young Socialist Revolutionary,
who had walked out of the Democratic Conference together with
the Bolsheviki that night when Tseretelly and the 'compromisers'
65   forced Coalition upon the democracy of Russia.
'You here?' I asked him.
His eyes flashed fire. 'Yes!' he cried. 'I left the Congress with
my party Wednesday night. I have not risked my life for twenty
years and more to submit now to the tyranny of the Dark People.
70   Their methods are intolerable. But they had not counted on the
peasants. . . . When the peasants begin to act then it is a question
of minutes before they are done for.'
'But the peasants – will they act? Doesn't the Land decree settle
the peasants? What more do they want?'
75   'Ah, the Land decree! It is our decree – it is the Socialist
Revolutionary programme intact! My party framed that policy,
after the most careful compilation of the wishes of the peasants
themselves. It is an outrage. . . .'
'But if it is your own policy, why do you object? If it is the
80   peasants' wishes, why will the people oppose it?'
'You don't understand! Don't you see that the peasants will
immediately realize that it is all a trick – that these usurpers have
stolen the Socialist Revolutionary programme?'

> Reed, op cit, pp 108–9

(e) Bolshevik Plans for the Peasants

The workers have been helping the poor peasants in their struggle
85   against the kulaks. In the civil war that has flared up in the
countryside the workers are on the side of the poor peasants, as

they were when they passed the S.R.-sponsored law on the socialisation of the land.

We Bolsheviks were opposed to this law. Yet we signed it,
90 because we did not want to oppose the will of the majority of peasants. The majority will is binding on us always, and to oppose the majority will is to betray the revolution.

We did not want to impose on the peasants the idea that the equal division of the land was useless, an idea which was alien to
95 them. Far better, we thought, if, by their own experience and suffering, the peasants themselves come to realise that equal division is nonsense. Only then could we ask them how they would escape the ruin and kulak domination that follow from the division of the land.

100 Division of the land was all very well as a beginning. Its purpose was to show that the land was being taken from the landowners and handed over to the peasants. But that is not enough. The solution lies only in socialised farming.

You did not realise this at the time, but you are coming round
105 to it by force of experience. They way to escape the disadvantages of small-scale farming lies in communes, cartels or peasant associations. That is the way to improve agriculture, economise forces and combat the kulaks, parasites and exploiters.

We were well aware that the peasants live rooted to the soil. The
110 peasants fear innovations and tenaciously cling to old habits. We knew the peasants would only believe in the benefits of any particular measure when their own common sense led them to understand and appreciate the benefits. And that is why we helped to divide the land, although we realised this was no solution.

115 Now the poor peasants themselves are beginning to agree with us. Experience is teaching them that while ten ploughs, say, are required when the land is divided into one hundred separate holdings, a smaller number suffices under communal farming because the land is not divided up so minutely. A commune permits
120 a whole cartel or association to make improvements in agriculture that are beyond the capacity of individual small owners, and so on.

Speech at a meeting of Peasant Delegates (8 November 1918)
Quoted in Lenin, *On the Alliance*, op cit, p 148

Questions

a What was the Bolshevik attitude to the land question in May 1917 – extract (a)?
b Who now owns the land, according to extract (b)?
c According to extract (c), why did Lenin give the land to the peasants?
d What do extracts (c) and (d) show about the strengths and weaknesses of the Bolshevik and Social Revolutionary parties?

e How does Lenin justify the Bolshevik change of policy over the land question, according to extract (e)?

(f) Problems in the country

This movement to the Right is observable, not only amongst the lower classes and workmen in the towns, but also amongst the peasants in the country districts. The latter are tired of endless committees, and are dissatisfied with the exorbitant prices payable
5 for manufactured goods. They would be content to see grain back at its pre-war price, if only they could satisfy their wants in clothes at a reasonable cost. They refuse to bring more grain to the market than is absolutely necessary. Their reason for this is that they do not wish to part with grain, which has a real value, in exchange
10 for paper money which has no value. They refuse to accept the latest issue of 20 and 40 rouble notes. They are, moreover, rich as a consequence of the war and high prices for grain and other farm products, and in no need of cash. All sales of instruments are now effected in ready money, for no credit is required. The deduction
15 from this is that if the peasants could be supplied by the Allies with goods, namely, boots, clothes, linen and cotton goods, and the other necessities of a peasant's life, then grain would be forthcoming in large quantities. The distribution of the goods could be carried out through the co-operative societies.
20 The furnishing of grain by the peasants would in itself be insufficient. It is necessary to provide means of transport by rail or water in order to bring it from the country districts to the army or the towns. It is this lack of transport which is preventing use being made of such grain supplies as are even now lying at the railway
25 stations. Monsieur Gerbel, who has recently been reappointed head of the grain supply Department in the Odessa Military district, and has just returned from a tour, reports that large quantities of grain are stored in the open, at roadside stations, and that they must either be moved or protection from the weather provided.

Public Record Office, Summary of Recent Events, FO 371 3000

(g) War Communism

30 In the transition period we shall carry out state purchases of grain and requisition grain surpluses. We know that only in this way shall we be able to do away with want and hunger. The vast majority of the workers suffer hardship because of the incorrect distribution of grain; to distribute it properly, the peasants must
35 deliver their quotas to the state as assessed, exactly, conscientiously, and without fail. Here Soviet power can make no concessions. This is not a matter of the workers' government fighting the peasants,

but an issue involving the very existence of socialism, the existence
of Soviet power. Today we cannot give the peasants any goods,
40 because there is a shortage of fuel and railway traffic is being held
up. We must start with the peasants lending the workers grain at
fixed prices, not at profiteering prices, so that the workers can
revive production. Every peasant will agree to this if it is a question
of an individual worker dying from starvation before his eyes. But
45 when millions of workers are in question, they do not understand
this and the old habits of profiteering gain the upper hand.

Speech at Conference on Party Work in the Countryside.
Quoted in Lenin, *On the Alliance*, op cit, p 148

(h) Problems with War Communism

The Food Commission of Ufa received a telegram from Inza that
a band of hungry 'partisans' had attacked a food train. They first
tore up the tracks and then opened fire on the train guard. They
50 were driven off, and the train reached Ruzaevka. . . .

In the beginning of March a small company of men was sent to
the village of T—— to requisition the bread reserves. When the
men arrived they were disarmed . . . by the peasants . . . . Another
company with two machine guns was sent, and they returned
55 without the machine guns. A third expedition was ordered out. . . .
At a given signal the peasants opened fire, killed six, and wounded
others. . . . A fourth and much better armed force was put into
the field. It arrested the local Soviet, recaptured the machine guns
and rifles. . . . Investigations are being made. . . .

60 News is arriving of the bread war which is taking place in
Voronezh, Smolensk, Tambov, Riazan, Simbirsk, Kursk, Khar-
kov, Ufa, Orenburg, and a number of other gubernias. Armed
detachments of Red Guards and hired soldiers are roaming over
villages and hamlets in quest of bread, making searches, laying
65 traps with more or less success. Sometimes they return with bread;
at other times they come back carrying the dead bodies of their
comrades who fell in the fight with the peasants. . . .

Many of the villages are now well armed, and seldom does a
bread expedition end without victims. . . . At the first report of a
70 requisitioning expedition the whole volost is mobilized . . . and
comes to the defense of the neighbouring village.

Voronezh has ten requisitioning companies, with a hundred
men in each, provided with machine guns, automobiles, and
bombs. . . .

75 In February there was a real battle at the station Muchkala. . . .
It is reported that several thousand people participated. . . .

At Smolensk two villages were wiped out and many peasants
and Red Guards were killed and wounded. . . .

The situation of the uezd and volost Soviets is not enviable. . . .

80 They are between two fires. . . . If they take the part of the
requisitioning gangs they are beaten by the peasants, and if they
protect the peasants they are pounced upon by the gubernia Soviets.
Recently one of the Soviets drove out the requisitioners and
immediately a punitive expedition was sent out and arrested the
85 Soviet.
The bread requisitioned does not always reach its destination.
Occasionally it is stolen on the way. . . . Trains are held up and
plundered. . . . Sometimes it takes two or three hundred men to
guard a train . . . . Many villages have organized gangs who attack
90 neighbouring villages and waylay people with food. . . .
Quoted in Bunyan and Fisher, op cit, p 664

Questions

a In extract (f), why did the peasants not bring more food to the
markets?
b What solutions to this problem are put forward in this extract?
c What is the policy of War Communism as outlined in extract
(g)?
d Was this policy hard to implement, according to extract (h)?
e What impressions do extracts (f), (g) and (h) give of agriculture
in Russia during the civil war?

3 Bolshevik Rule

(a) Lenin and the press

Although Messrs. Lenin and Trotsky show no signs of yielding in
essentials, they have been subjected to continuous criticism from
every side for their policy of thorough and, as regards the press,
they have thought it expedient to modify their attitude. For some
5 days, no papers were allowed to be printed except pure Bolshevik
journals; then some other Socialist papers appeared, and now most
of the old newspapers are published, though sometimes under a
new name. A hot debate took place in the Soviet on November
17th on this subject and Trotsky and Lenin laid down the doctrine
10 that the old idea of property now belonged to the Soviets and that
the old idea of the liberty of the Press was as out of date as was
that of private property. The Press must be controlled by Socialists
and no advertisements would be permitted save in Soviet papers.
The application of this doctrine, which was accepted by the Soviet,
15 has been temporarily postponed owing to the attitude of the
typesetters' union who had declared they will set up any papers
they choose, whether authorized by the Commissaries of the people
or not.
Public Record Office, Summary of Recent Events,
FO 371 3000

(b) Suppression of hostile newspapers

Everyone knows that the bourgeois press is one of the mighty
20 weapons of the bourgeoisie. In a critical time like this, when the
new Workers' and Peasants' Government is just getting started, it
is not possible to leave in the hands of the enemy a weapon no less
dangerous than bombs and machine guns. This is why temporary
and special measures were taken to stop the flow of mud and lies
25 from the young victory of the people. . . . The Soviet of the
People's Commissars decrees that: (a) Those organs of the press
will be closed which a) call for open opposition or disobedience to
the Workers' and Peasants' Government; b) sow sedition by a
frankly slanderous perversion of facts; c) encourage deeds of a
30 manifestly criminal character. . . .

The above regulations are of a temporary nature and will be
removed by a special decree just as soon as normal conditions are
re-established.

> Degree of Sovnarkom, 9 November 1917. Quoted in
> Bunyan and Fisher, op cit, p 670

(c) Red Terror

The murder of Volodarsky, the murder of Uritzky, the attempt to
35 murder and the wounding of the President of the Council of
People's Commissars, Vladimir Ilyitch Lenin, the mass shooting
of tens of thousands of our comrades in Finland, in Ukraina and,
finally on the Don, and in Czecho–Slavia the constant discovery of
plots in the rear of our army, the open implication of Right Socialist
40 Revolutionaries and other counter–revolutionary scoundrels in these
plots, and at the same time the extremely negligible number of
serious repressions and mass shootings of the White Guards and
the bourgeoisie by the Soviets, all this shows that, notwithstanding
constant words about mass terror against the Socialist Revolution-
45 aries, the White Guards and the bourgeoisie, this terror really does
not exist.

There must emphatically be an end of such a situation. There
must be an immediate end of looseness and tenderness. All Right
Socialist Revolutionaries who are known to local Soviets must be
50 arrested immediately. Considerable numbers of hostages must be
taken from among the bourgeoisie and the officers. At the least
attempt at resistance or the least movement among the White
Guards mass shooting must be inflicted without hesitation. The local
Provincial Executive Committees must display special initiative in
55 this direction.

The departments of administration, through the militia, and the
Extraordinary Commissions must take all measures to detect and
arrest all persons who are hiding under assumed names and must

shoot without fail all who are implicated in White Guard activity.
60   All the above mentioned measures must be carried out immediately.

> Order for Red Terror (4 September 1918). Quoted in
> Chamberlain, vol II, op cit, pp 470–6

(d) Trotsky on terror

The working class, which seized power in battle, had as its object and its duty to establish that power unshakeably, to guarantee its own supremacy beyond question, to destroy its enemies' hankering
65   for a new revolution, and thereby to make sure of carrying out Socialist reforms. Otherwise there would be no point in seizing power.

The revolution 'logically' does not demand terrorism just as 'logically' it does not demand an armed insurrection. What a
70   profound commonplace! But the revolution does require of the revolutionary class that it should attain its end by all methods at its disposal – if necessary, by an armed rising; if required, by terrorism. A revolutionary class which has conquered power with arms in its hands is bound to, and will, suppress, rifle in hand, all attempts to
75   tear the power out of its hands. Where it has against it a hostile army, it will oppose to it its own army. Where it is confronted with armed conspiracy, attempt at murder, or rising, it will hurl at the heads of its enemies an unsparing penalty.

> Leon Trotsky, *In Defence of Terrorism*. Quoted in Sidney
> Hook, *Marx and the Marxists* (Princeton, NJ, 1955) pp
> 205–6

(e) The formation of the Cheka

To fight the external foe there was organized a Red Guard, which
80   later became the Red Army. To fight the internal foe it was necessary to create an organ . . . that would protect the rear of the Red Army and permit the peaceful development of the Soviet form of government. Such an organ was the Extraordinary Commission to Fight Counter-Revolution and Sabotage. Later on its functions
85   were enlarged to include negligence of duty, profiteering, and banditry.

The Commission itself (composed at that time of Dzerzhinsky, Ksenofontov, Averin, Sergo, Peterson, Peters, Evseev, and Trifonov) outlines its duties as follows: To cut off at the roots all
90   counter-revolution and sabotage in Russia; to hand over to the revolutionary court all who are guilty of such attempts; to work out measures for dealing with such cases; and to enforce these measures without mercy. . . . It was necessary to make the foe feel that there was everywhere about him a seeing eye and a heavy

95 hand ready to come down on him the moment he undertook
anything against the Soviet Government.

Quoted in Bunyan and Fisher, op cit, pp 495–6

Questions

a Why should the press be controlled, in extract (a)?
b How effective is this control, according to this extract?
c Compare the reasons for press control outlined in extracts (a)
   and (b).
★ · d What do these two extracts reveal about the nature of Bolshevik
        government?
★   e Analyse the arguments in favour of a Red Terror outlined in
        extracts (c) and (d).
    f What was the purpose of the Cheka, according to extract (e)?

VIII   The Last Years of Lenin

Introduction

The successful conclusion to the civil war saw a marked change in communist policy. During the conflict both workers and peasants had been pushed to the limit. This policy of War Communism had not pleased them. A symbolic blow came with the revolt of the long-time vanguard of the Bolshevik Party, the sailors of Kornstadt, who were protesting at government policy. Lenin accepted that the people had been overworked and that this policy could not continue in peacetime. This was not just giving in to pressure; it had already been proved that War Communism did not work, at least as far as agriculture was concerned. At the same time, Lenin had no hesitation in crushing the Kronstadt rebellion, having totally ignored the demands for free elections and a lessening of censorship. The New Economic Policy brought back a stable currency and stopped the forcible seizure of foodstuffs from the countryside. Both peasants and workers were encouraged to produce goods for personal profit. The Bolsheviks claimed they held the 'Commanding Heights' of heavy industry and still looked for major changes in the long run; but temporarily it was one step backwards from communism.

This is one of the problems as regards any assessment of Lenin and the revolution for the latter was not complete when Lenin died. The revolution necessitated a complete change. It was not enough for the Bolsheviks just to seize power; they also had to effect a complete change of hearts and minds of the people and force them to be free, to accept new ideas of equality and communal living. Lenin accepted this would take time. The NEP showed that, at the time, self-interest was still dominant. This policy made the government popular again. There is nothing to suggest that Lenin had abandoned his long-term goals, or that he would hesitate in the future to enforce unpopular policies, notably the collectivisation of the land. The Bolshevik Party had already created the preconditions for strong rule but if the Communists dominated Russia, then Lenin dominated the party. So strong was his influence that there would obviously be a very different style of government once he had gone.

1 New Policies in Peacetime

(a) Rescuing White Russians

May, 1920   H.M.S. IN THE BLACK SEA.
Among other duties now falling to the lot of our men-of-war is
that of rescuing South Russian troops and refugees from the tender
mercies of the Bolsheviks.

5   One by one the towns and villages along the narrow coast roads
skirting the Black Sea are falling into the hands of the Bolsheviks,
and some distance ahead of the latter's advance swarm the retreating
volunteers and those of the population who shrink from the Red
occupation. The majority of these refugees are Cossack irregulars
10   and tribesmen, others are local landowners with their retainers, and
the remainder are ex-officers, women and middle-class people who
succeeded in escaping from Petrograd and Moscow in the early
days of the revolution.

The first place to which we gave assistance, was a beautiful
15   summer resort, very like Folkestone, and here we found the
Bolsheviks trying to cross a burning bridge whilst the refugees and
the White Army were retreating in confusion on the other side.
We closed in to the shore and took on board 600 wounded and 200
women and children, while firing went on from the hills. It took
20   the greater part of a day, and then we sailed for a part of the Crimea
about 250 miles away. The wounded were in a dreadful state:
Generals' and Colonels' wives and children in the ward-room, and
they numbered about 70 to each meal. All the decks were strewn
with soldiers too weak to stand, and the men were splendid in
25   looking after them. Many of the officers gave up their cabins for
the women, and four had the use of mine.

. . . We took 1,500 on board, and the ship was in the most
crowded state imaginable. Luckily, these people were disciplined
troops and unwounded, so we did not have so much trouble as the
30   last time. There were a few women of the upper classes, but no
peasants or children. Some were strikingly pretty women, dressed
in officer uniform, who have been fighting in the trenches – one
of them for three years, and twice wounded. They were very
picturesque and were well educated, speaking perfect French, and
35   they still manage to powder their faces and manicure their nails!
The women officers have a special bodyguard of men, who simply
worship them and have sworn to protect them to the death. All of
them were very grateful to us, and they played and sang 'God save
the King.'

King Edward's School, Bath, *The Edwardian Magazine* (May
1920)

(b) Popular complaints

40 I inquired about their work, their lives, and their attitude toward the new decrees. 'As if we had not been driven enough before,' complained one of the men. 'Now we are to work under the military nagaika [whip]. Of course, we will have to be in the shop or they will punish us as industrial deserters. But how can they get
45 more work out of us? We are suffering hunger and cold. We have no strength to give more.' I suggested that the Government was probably compelled to introduce such methods, and that if Russian industry were not revived the condition of the workers would grow even worse. Besides, the Putilov men were receiving the
50 preferred 'payok'. 'We understand the great misfortune that has befallen Russia,' one of the workers replied, 'but we cannot squeeze more out of ourselves. Even the two pounds of bread we are getting is not enough. Look at the bread,' he said, holding up a black crust; 'can we live on that? And our children? If not for our
55 people in the country or some trading on the market we would die altogether.'

'But what can the Government do in the face of the food shortage?' I asked. 'Food shortage!' the man exclaimed; 'look at the markets. Did you see any shortage of food there? Speculation
60 and the new bourgeoisie, that's what's the matter. The one-man management is our new slave driver. First the bourgeoisie sabotaged us, and now they are again in control.'

Emma Goldman, *My Disillusionment in Russia* (New York, 1918) pp 82–3

(c) The demands of the Kronstadt sailors

Having heard the report of the representatives of the Crews, despatched by the General Meeting of the Crews from the ships to
65 Petrograd in order to learn the state of affairs in Petrograd we decided:
1. In view of the fact that the present Soviets do not represent the will of the workers and peasants, immediately to re-elect the Soviets by secret voting, with free preliminary agitation among all workers
70 and peasants before the elections.
2. Freedom of speech and press for workers, peasants, Anarchists and Left Socialist Parties.
3. Freedom of meetings, trade-unions and peasant associations.
4. To convene, not later than March 1, 1921, a nonparty conference
75 of workers, soldiers and sailors of Petrograd City, Kronstadt and Petrograd Province.
5. To liberate all political prisoners of Socialist Parties, and also all workers, peasants, soldiers and sailors who have been imprisoned in connection with working class and peasant movements.

80 6. To elect a commission to review the cases of those who are imprisoned in jails and concentration camps.

7. To abolish all Political Departments, because no single party may enjoy privileges in the propaganda of its ideas and receive funds from the state for this purpose. Instead of these Departments
85 locally elected cultural–educational commissions must be established and supported by the state.

8. All 'cordon detachments' are to be abolished immediately.

9. To equalize rations for all workers, harmful departments being excepted.
90 10. To abolish all Communist fighting detachments in all military units, and also various Communist guards at factories. If such detachments and guards are needed they may be chosen from the companies in military units and in the factories according to the judgement of the workers.
95 11. To grant the peasant full right to do what he sees fit with his land and also to possess cattle, which he must maintain and manage with his own strength, but without employing hired labor.

Quoted in Chamberlin, vol II, op cit, pp 495–6

(d) Lenin and Kronstadt

The fact that the enemies of the proletariat take advantage of all deviations from a strictly consistent communist line was seen most
100 clearly in the example of the Kronstadt uprising, when the bourgeois counter-revolution and White Guards in all the world's countries immediately manifested their readiness to accept even slogans favouring a Soviet system, if only the dictatorship of the proletariat could be overthrown in Russia; when the Socialist Revolutionaries
105 and the bourgeois counter-revolution in general made use, in Kornstadt, of slogans allegedly favouring an uprising in favour of a Soviet system but opposed to the Soviet government in Russia. Such instances fully prove that the White Guardists are striving – and are able – to assume the guise of communists and even to
110 assume positions to the 'left' of communism, if only they can weaken and overthrow the bulwark of the proletarian revolution in Russia. The Menshevik leaflets in Petrograd on the eve of the Kronstadt uprising show in the same way how the Mensheviks were using differences within the RKP in order, by deeds, to incite
115 and support the Kronstadt rebels, Socialist Revolutionaries, and White Guardists.

Quoted in Elwood, vol 2, op cit, p 119

Questions

a   What types of people are rescued by the ship in extract (a)?

b   Is the author of extract (a) sympathetic towards the refugees?

   c What complaints are levelled against the Communist government in extracts (b) and (c)?

★ *d* How valid are the criticisms outlined in extract (c)?

   e According to extract (d), why was Lenin worried by the Kronstadt uprising?

★ *f* Why was it significant that the Kronstadt sailors started this rebellion?

(e) A new policy

It was not a surprise to me when Lenin declared his new economic policy. Of course, a man of such tenacity would never have given the signal for 'economic retreat', which meant in plain words a retreat from Communism, until he was compelled to, and there
5 were already signs enough that the evolution of the country was going dead against his theory. This retreat came of itself with the victory in war over the Whites and their allies. Till then, Soviet Russia was like a beseiged city and could only have a hand to mouth policy, in economics as in anything else; and beseiged cities
10 often perforce approach Communism. But directly they had won their war, the Communists had to recognise the wholesale economic breakdown caused by the wholesale application of their theory, and the facts were faced very sincerely by the then Commissary of Industry, Rykov, in a report to a Congress of National Economic
15 Councils in Moscow in January 1920 – the factory workers in employment who were supposed to be chief gainers by factory output to fifteen per cent. Though the system had been applied during a civil war, this was, and was meant to be, not merely war Communism, such as is appropriate to a beseiged city, but militant
20 Communism or rather pure Communism, and its failure was self-evident. The Government soon went full circle; and the workers' control was replaced by labour conscription. In fact, Russia could not have lasted out even these three years under pure Communism unless she had been a predominantly agricultural country to which
25 the system could hardly be applied.

      Bernard Pares, *My Russian Memoirs* (1931) pp 585–6

(f) The New Economic Policy

NEP (New Economic Policy) – the policy of the proletarian state during the period of transition from capitalism to socialism. This policy was 'new' in contrast to the economic policy which had been conducted in Soviet Russia during the period of foreign
30 military intervention and the civil war, which went down in history as the policy of War Communism (1918–20). The latter was called forth by war-time conditions, and its characteristic features were extreme centralisation of production and distribution, prohibition

of free trading, and food requisitioning which compelled the
peasants to turn in all surplus produce to the state.

When the New Economic Policy was adopted, commodity-
money relations became the basic link between socialist industry
and the small peasant economy. When food requisitioning was
abolished and replaced by the tax in kind, the peasants were able
to dispose of their surplus produce as they chose, i.e., sell their
surpluses on the market and through the market obtain the industrial
goods they required.

The New Economic Policy was calculated to achieve a firm
economic and political alliance between the working class and the
peasantry for the building of socialism, for the development of
productive forces along socialist lines. It provided for a certain
measure of capitalism while the basic economic positions remained
in the hands of the proletarian state. It involved the struggle of the
socialist elements against the capitalist elements, assuming the
ultimate victory of the socialist elements, the eliminations of the
exploiting classes, and the successful building of socialism in the
U.S.S.R.

Lenin, *The October Revolution*, op cit, pp 406–7

(g) Lenin on the changes (i)

The proletarian state must become a cautious, assiduous and shrewd
'businessman', a punctilious wholesale merchant – otherwise it will
never succeed in putting this small–peasant country economically
on its feet. Under existing conditions, living as we are side by side
with the capitalist (for the time being capitalist) West, there is no
other way of progressing to communism. A wholesale merchant
seems to be an economic type as remote from communism as
heaven from earth. But that is one of the contradictions which, in
actual life, lead from a small-peasant economy via state capitalism
to socialism. Personal incentive will step up production; we must
increase production first and foremost and at all costs. Wholesale
trade economically unites millions of small peasants: it gives them
a personal incentive, links them up and leads them to the next step,
namely, to various forms of association and alliance in the process
of production itself.

4th Anniversary of the October Revolution. Quoted in ibid,
pp 338–9

(h) Lenin on the changes (ii)

So far we have handled things very, very badly in this field, as we
must frankly admit. We must recognise this shortcoming and not
gloss over it; we must do everything possible to eliminate it and
understand that the foundation of our New Economic Policy lies

in this alliance. There are only two ways in which proper relations between the working class and the peasants can be established. If large-scale industry is flourishing, if it can immediately supply the small peasants with a sufficient amount of goods, or more than previously, and in this way establish proper relations between manufactured goods and the supply of surplus agricultural goods coming from the peasants, then the peasants, the non–Party peasants, will acknowledge, by virtue of experience, that this new system is better than the capitalist system. We speak of a flourishing large-scale industry, which is able to supply all the goods the peasants are in urgent need of, and this possibility exists.

9th Congress of Soviets (23–28 December 1921). Quoted in Lenin, *The Alliance*, op cit, p 182

Questions

a Why did the Communists adopt a new policy, according to extract (e)?
b How critical of communism is this extract?
c What were the differences between War Communism and the New Economic Policy according to extract (f)?
★ *d* How 'communist' are the arguments outlined in extract (g)?
e What do extracts (g) and (h) reveal about the political skills of Lenin?

(i) Industry

The basic lever of the New Economic Policy is considered to be trade turnover. Correct relations between the proletariat and the peasantry and the creation of a completely new form of economic union between these two classes for the period of transition from capitalism to socialism are not possible without the establishment of a regular exchange of goods or products between industry and agriculture.

In particular, the achievement of an exchange of goods is necessary as a stimulus to the expansion of peasants' sown areas and to an improvement of peasant agriculture.

Enterprise and initiative at the local level must be comprehensively supported and developed at all costs. . . .

Support is to be given to small and medium-sized (both private and co-operative) enterprises, chiefly to those that do not require supplying with raw materials, fuel, and foodstuffs from state stocks.

The renting of state enterprises to private persons, co-operatives, cartels, and partnerships is to be permitted. Local economic agencies have the authority to conclude such contracts without permission from higher authorities. It is mandatory that the Council of Labour and Defence be informed in each such case.

There is to be a review (to a definite extent) of the production programmes of large-scale industry in the sense of stepping up the output of consumer goods and those goods commonly used by peasants.

25　　There is to be an expansion of independence and initiative of every major enterprise in holding the financial means and material resources at its disposal. A corresponding, clear-cut resolution is to be introduced for approval by the Sovnarkom.

> Resolution on Economic Policy (27 May 1921). Quoted in Elwood, vol 2, op cit, p 138

(j) Communist plans for agriculture

The formation of the Poor Peasants' Committees and this joint
30　　congress of land departments, Poor Peasants' Committees and agricultural communes, taken in conjunction with the struggle which took place in the countryside this summer and autumn, go to show that very many peasants have been awakened, and that the peasants themselves, the majority of the working peasants, are
35　　striving toward collective farming. Of course, I repeat, we must tackle this great reform gradually. Here, nothing can be done at one stroke. But I must remind you that the fundamental law on the socialisation of the land, whose adoption was a foregone conclusion on the first day after the Revolution of October 25, at
40　　the very first session of the first organ of Soviet power, the Second All-Russia Congress of Soviets, did more than abolish private ownership of land for ever and do away with landed estates. It also stipulated, among other things, that farm property, draught animals and farm implements which passed into the possession of
45　　the nation and the working peasants should become public property and cease to be the private property of individual farms. And on the fundamental question of our present aims, of what tasks of land disposal we want carried out, and what we want from the supporters of the Soviet government, the working peasants, in this respect,
50　　Article 11 of the law on the socialisation of the land, which was adopted in February 1918, states that the aim is to develop collective farming, the most advantageous form of farming from the point of view of economy of labour and products. This will be at the expense of individual farming and with the aim of passing over to
55　　socialist farming.

> Speech to the Congress of Land Departments (11 December 1918). Quoted in Lenin, *The October Revolution*, op cit, pp 266–7

Questions

a What did the New Economic Policy mean as far as industry was concerned, according to extract (i)?

★ b Did the NEP benefit the peasants and industrial workers equally?

c What future plans did Lenin have for the land, according to extract (j)?

★ d To what extent was the NEP a regressive step?

2 Communist Government

(a) Lenin and Trotsky

Later I was to acquire a considerable respect for his intellectual capacity, but at that moment I was more impressed by his tremendous will-power, his relentless determination, and his lack of emotion. He furnished a complete antithesis to Trotsky, who,
5   strangely silent, was also present at our interview. Trotsky was all temperament – an individualist and an artist, on whose vanity even I could play with some success. Lenin was impersonal and almost inhuman. His vanity was proof against all flattery. The only appeal that one could make to him was to his sense of humour, which if
10   sardonic, was highly developed. During the next few months I was to be pestered with various requests from London to verify rumours of serious dissensions between Lenin and Trotsky – dissensions from which our Government hoped much. I could have given the answer after that first interview. Trotsky was a great
15   organiser and a man of immense physical ccourage. But, morally, he was as incapable of standing against Lenin as a flea would be against an elephant. In the Council of Commissars there was not a man who did not consider himself the equal of Trotsky. There was not a Commissar who did not regard Lenin as a demi-god, whose
20   decisions were to be accepted without question. Squabbles among the Commissars were frequent, but they never touched Lenin.

I remember Chicherin giving me an account of a Soviet Cabinet meeting. Trotsky would bring forward a proposal. It would be violently opposed by another Commissar. Endless discussion would
25   follow, and all the time Lenin would be writing notes on his knee, his attention concentrated on some work of his own. At last someone would say: 'Let Vladimir Illyitch [Lenin's Christian name and patronymic] decide.' Lenin would look up from his work, give his decision in one sentence, and all would be peace.

Lockhart, op cit, p 238

(b) The role of the Communist Party

30   The Communist Party is part of the working class: its most

progressive, most classconscious and therefore most revolutionary part. The Communist Party is created by means of selection of the best, most classconscious, most self-sacrificing and farsighted workers. The Communist Party has no interests which are different
35 from those of the working class. The Communist Party is distinguished from the whole mass of the workers because it surveys the historical road of the working class as a whole and attempts at all the turningpoints of this road to defend the interests of the working class as a whole, not of separate groups and trades. The
40 Communist Party is the lever of political organization, with the help of which the more progressive part of the working class directs on the right paths the whole mass of the proletariat and the semi-proletariat.

2nd Congress of the Communist International 1920. Quoted in Chamberlain, vol II, op cit, p 361

(c) Communist support

I have been speaking too long as it is; hence I wish to say only a
45 few words about the concept of 'masses'. It is one that changes in accordance with the changes in the nature of the struggle. At the beginning of the struggle it took only a few thousand genuinely revolutionary workers to warrant talk of the masses. If the party succeeds in drawing into the struggle not only its own members,
50 if it also succeeds in arousing non-party people, it is well on the way to winning the masses. During our revolutions there were instances when several thousand workers represented the masses. In the history of our movement, and of our struggle against the Mensheviks, you will find many examples, where several thousand
55 workers in a town were enough to give a clearly mass character to the movement. You have a mass when several thousand non-party workers, who usually live in a philistine life and drag out a miserable existence, and who have never heard anything about politics, begin to act in a revolutionary way. If the movement spreads and
60 intensifies, it gradually develops into a real revolution. We saw this in 1905 and 1917 during three revolutions, and you too will have to go through all this. When the revolution has been sufficiently prepared, the concept 'masses' becomes different: several thousand workers no longer constitute the masses. This word begins to
65 denote something else. The concept of 'masses' undergoes a change so that it implies the majority, and not simply a majority of the workers alone, but the majority of all the exploited.

3rd Congress of the Communist International. Quoted in Lenin, *The October Revolution*, op cit, pp 318–19

a How are Lenin and Trotsky compared in extract (a)?

b What does this extract have to say about the style of communist government under Lenin?

c What was the role of the Communist Party according to extract (b)?

d How has the concept of 'masses' changed in extract (c)?

e How popular were the Bolsheviks during the period 1917–24?

3 Assessments of the Revolution

(a) Lenin's official version

Let us recall the main stages of our revolution. The first stage, the purely political stage, so to speak, from October 25 to January 5, when the Constituent Assembly was dissolved. In a matter of ten weeks we did a hundred times more to actually and completely
5 destroy the survivals of feudalism in Russia than the Mensheviks and Socialist-Revolutionaries did during the eight months they were in power from February to October 1917. At that time, the Mensheviks and Socialist-Revolutionaries in Russia, and all the heroes of the Two-and-a-Half International abroad, acted as miser-
10 able accomplices of reaction. As for the anarchists, some stood aloof in perplexity, while others helped us. Was the revolution a bourgeois revolution at that time? Of course it was, insofar as our function was to complete the bourgeois-democratic revolution, insofar as there was as yet no class struggle among 'peasantry'.
15 But, at the same time, we accomplished a great deal over and above the bourgeois revolution for the socialist, proletarian revolution: (1) we developed the forces of the working class for its utilisation of state power to an extent never achieved before; (2) we struck a blow that was felt all over the world against the fetishes of petty-
20 bourgeois democracy, the Constituent Assembly and bourgeois 'liberties' such as freedom of the press for the rich; (3) we created the Soviet type of state, which was a gigantic step in advance of 1793 and 1871.

The second stage. The Brest-Litovsk peace. There was a riot of
25 revolutionary phrase-mongering against peace – the semi-jingoist phrase-mongering of the Socialist-Revolutionaries and Mensheviks, and the 'Left' phrase-mongering of a certain section of the Bolsheviks. 'Since you have made peace with imperialism you are doomed,' argued the philistines, some in panic and some with
30 malicious glee. But the Socialist-Revolutionaries and the Mensheviks made peace with imperialism as participants in the bourgeois robbery of the workers. We 'made peace', surrendering to the robbers part of our property, only in order to save the workers'

rule, and in order to be able to strike heavier blows at the robbers
35 later on. At that time we heard no end of talk about our having
'lost faith in the forces of the working class'; but we did not allow
ourselves to be deceived by this phrase-mongering.

The third stage. The Civil War, beginning with the Czechoslovaks and the Constituent Assembly crowd and ending with
40 Wrangel, from 1918 to 1920. At the beginning of the war our Red
Army was non-existent. Judged as a material force, this army is
even now insignificant compared with the army of any of the
Entente powers. The alliance between the peasants and the workers
led by proletarian rule – this achievement of epoch-making
45 importance – was raised to an unprecedented level. The Mensheviks
and Socialist-Revolutionaries acted as the accomplices of the monarchy overtly (as Ministers, organisers and propagandists) and ·
covertly (the more 'subtle' and despicable method adopted by the
Chernovs and Martovs, who pretended to wash their hands of the
50 affair but actually used their pens against us). The anarchists too
vacillated helplessly, one section of them helping us, while another
hindering us by their clamour against military discipline or by their
scepticism.

The fourth stage. The Entente is compelled to cease (for how
55 long?) its intervention and blockade. Our unprecedentedly dislo-
cated country is just barely beginning to recover, is only just
realising the full depth of its ruin, is suffering the most terrible
hardships – stoppage of industry, crop failures, famine, epidemics.

New Times and Old Mistakes in a New Guise. Quoted in
Lenin, *The October Revolution*, op cit, pp 326–7

Questions

a   What criticisms are levelled against the Mensheviks and Social
Revolutionaries in extract (a)?
b   What does this extract have to say about the bourgeois and
proletarian revolutions?
c   What are the achievements of the communist revolution according to this extract?

(b) A communist critic

Bolshevism has, up to the present, triumphed in Russia, but
Socialism has already suffered a defeat. We have only to look at
the form of society which has developed under the Bolshevik
regime, and which was bound so to develop, as soon as the
5   Bolshevik method was applied.
. . .
Originally they were whole-hearted protagonists of a National
Assembly, ·elected on the strength of a universal and equal vote.

But they set this aside, as soon as it stood in their way. They were thoroughgoing opponents of the death penalty, yet they established a bloody rule. When democracy was being abandoned in the state they became fiery upholders of democracy within the proletariat, but they are repressing this democracy more and more by means of their personal dictatorship. They abolished the piece-work system, and are now reintroducing it. At the beginning of their regime they declared it to be their object to smash the bureaucratic apparatus, which represented the means of power of the old State; but they have introduced in its place a new form of the bureaucratic rule. They came into power by dissolving the discipline of the army, and finally the army itself. They have created a new army, severely disciplined. They strove to reduce all classes to the same level, instead of which they have called into being a new class distinction. They have created a class which stands on a lower level than the proletariat, which latter they have raised to a privileged class; and over and above this they have caused still another class to appear, which is in receipt of large incomes and enjoys high privileges.

Karl Kautsky, *Terrorism and Communism* (1920) p 215

(c) A German communist

We demand democracy based on the principle of the equality of all men. Bolshevism sets up a dictatorship resting on the inequality and absolute rightlessness of those who do not belong to it.

We demand the right of free opinion. In Bolshevik Russia, every non-Bolshevik, even a democrat or socialist, is outlawed as a 'counter-revolutionary.'

We demand a justice resting on humane sentiments. Bolshevism perpetrates mass-executions, and has even reintroduced torture.

We demand the inviolability of the individual, and of his rights of property in objects of daily use, which belong to him even in a socialist state. In Bolshevist Russia, there are no legal guarantees against the arbitrary acts of a ruling clique; and not only are land, factories, mines, &c., expropriated, but even the coat, the bed, the armchair of the individual.

We want to transform the capitalist economic order into a socialistic one. Bolshevism has made out of the economic life of Russia a desert in which nothing grows.

We demand the right of everyone to work and to just pay. Bolshevism has to a large degree 'sabotaged' the factories so that there is neither work nor wages.

We demand bread for the masses, but Bolshevism cannot even guarantee them the exiguous ration of the days of capitalism.

We demand the education of the people to a higher intellectual culture. This, however, can only be realised on the basis of material welfare. Nothing is effected by merely putting up a statue to Marx, as the Bolsheviks have done.

Quoted in Wilcox, op cit, p 290

(d) A British critic

They say that the horrors are at bottom the fault of the Old Regime,
which kept the Russian people in ignorance and degradation; that
55 the Terror was not adopted by the Bolsheviks till it had been
used against them by the Social-Revolutionaries; that the whole
economic fabric of the country had been shaken to its very
foundations before Lenin came into power. In short, they urge that
what is generally understood to be Bolshevism is not really
60 Bolshevism at all, but the results of extraneous and accidental
circumstances which have no necessary connection with its principles.

    To the sceptics – those who do not believe in the promises of
Bolshevism – it can only appear as one of the greatest scourges
65 that have ever afflicted humanity. To everything that was bad in
the Tsardom, it has paid the tribute of imitation; and the wrongs
of the new tyranny have been infinitely worse than those of the
old. No Tsar of modern times rules so autocratically as Lenin, and
none was more ruthless. The Tsars restricted freedom of speech –
70 Lenin has absolutely abolished it. The Tsars suppressed this or that
newspaper – Lenin allows none which opposes his views. The
Tsars put people to death for offences which existed only in Russia –
Lenin has massacred thousands against whom no charge at all was
brought. No more damning judgement could be passed upon Lenin
75 than the words he used against the Tsars for doing what he has
now done himself. And, by a strange irony of fate, he attempted
to justify his actions by exactly the same pleas as have always been
put forward by tyrants when they have deigned to put forward
any at all. The people, he said, were not yet capable of distinguishing
80 between truth and falsehood, so that authority had to decide what
they might hear and what they might read.

Ibid, p 291

(e) The evil empire?

But Russia had fallen by the way; and in falling she had changed
her identity. An apparition with countenance different from any
yet seen on earth stood in the place of the old Ally. We saw a state
85 without a nation, an army without a country, a religion without a
God. The Government which claimed to be the new Russia sprang
from Revolution and was fed by Terror. It had denounced the faith
of treaties; it had made a separate peace; it had released a million
Germans for the final onslaught in the West. It had declared that

90 between itself and non-communist society no good faith, public or
private, could exist and no engagements need be respected. It had
repudiated alike all that Russia owed and all that was owing to her.
Just when the worst was over, when victory was in sight, when
the fruits of measureless sacrifice were at hand, the old Russia had
95 been dragged down, and in her place there ruled 'the nameless
beast' so long foretold in Russian legend. Thus the Russian people
were deprived of Victory, Honour, Freedom, Peace and Bread.
Thus there was to be no Russia in the Councils of the Allies – only
an abyss which still continues in human affairs.

Churchill, op cit, p 71

Questions

a What criticisms are levelled against the Bolsheviks in extract
(b)?

★ b Analyse the assertions in extracts (a), (b) and (c) that the
revolution in Russia was not a truly communist one.

c How is communist rule compared to that of the tsar in extract
(d)?

d Why might other countries distrust communist Russia according
to extract (e)?

★ e Using these extracts and other information known to you, how
complete was the communist revolution by the death of Lenin
in 1924?